Y0-BDA-609

A Sensory Approach to the Curriculum

for pupils with profound and multiple learning difficulties

JUDY DAVIS

WITHDRAWN
WRIGHT STATE UNIVERSITY LIBRARIES

David Fulton Publishers
London

LC
4036
.G7
D38
2001

David Fulton Publishers Ltd
Ormond House, 26–27 Boswell Street, London WC1N 3JZ

www.fultonpublishers.co.uk

First published in Great Britain by David Fulton Publishers 2001

Note: The right of Judy Davis to be identified as the author of this work has been asserted by her in accordance with the Copyright, Designs and Patents Act 1988.

Copyright © Judy Davis 2001

British Library Cataloguing in Publication Data
A catalogue record for this book is available from the British Library.

ISBN 1-85346-671-9

All rights reserved. No part of this publication may be reproduced, stored in a retrieval system or transmitted, in any form, or by any means, electronic, mechanical, photocopying, recording or otherwise, without the prior permission of the publishers.

The publishers would like to thank Yvonne Messenger for copy-editing and Sheila Harding for proofreading this book.

Typeset by Textype Typesetters, Cambridge
Printed by Bell & Bain Ltd, Glasgow

Contents

Acknowledgements

Initial encouragement to write this book came from my tutor, Barbara Doyle, and from Geoff Jones, who was at the time the senior inspector and monitoring inspector for special schools in Oxfordshire. David Fulton and his colleagues had the faith to convert the idea into reality, and my husband, Ian, has provided ongoing support during the difficult periods. Without this backing team I may not have persevered.

I also want to thank colleagues from Mabel Prichard School and the Ormerod School for all we have shared together over the years and for passing on their knowledge and experience. Other people have allowed me to work with them, observe them in action, draw on their special expertise and spend their valuable time. In particular I would like to mention Nicola Grove, Sarah Blundell, Michael Thompson, Bobbie Stormont, Hilary Wainer, Ann Brown, Rhiannon Prys-Owen and Caroline Astell-Burt.

Last but not least, I dedicate this book to the pupils who inspired it, and to their parents who gave me nothing but encouragement and support over the years. Writing has brought back happy memories of my time with Aveline, Brian, Chloe, Lisa, Louise, Michelle, Paul, Jamie, Jonathan A., Jonathan H. and Sanela, to name a few. It is for other children and young people with similar difficulties that this book has been written.

Introduction

An interactive approach (to teaching) . . . is based on intrinsic motivation, rather than extrinsic reward. It is not the learner who fails to learn but the teacher who fails to provide an adequate learning opportunity.

Collis and Lacey (1996 p. 13)

Watch any group of children playing on the beach. They will be totally absorbed in what they are doing and completely unaware of how hard they are working and what they are learning – but learning they certainly are! It is revealing to look at the subjects in the curriculum with the range of skills, knowledge and understanding pupils are encouraged to acquire, and to discover the rich learning environment provided by the seaside.

Some children will be playing on their own, lost in imaginative play, exploring rock pools or making patterns with shells and pebbles. Others will be working in groups, interacting, discussing, making plans and exchanging ideas for building sand castles that will resist the tide, or inventing new games. These activities may develop into dramas with children taking turns at listening to others or taking the lead.

Young children will be learning about 'number' as they count their collections of pebbles, shells and sea glass to see who has the most, or sort them into groups. Concepts of shape, space and measurement will be involved as they fill buckets with sand and water, make a variety of sand castles, dig holes and play hop-scotch on the sand. There is no end to the possibilities for learning about science as children observe, explore and investigate what will happen when water is poured into a hole in the sand, whether wet or dry sand is better for building, which materials are best for making a boat, or what happened to make 'sea glass' so smooth. They will learn about different sea creatures and what they need to survive, and notice the variety of seaweed – smooth and slimy when wet and crisp when dry, or bumpy and fun to pop. They will look at the different colours in pebbles, glass and shells, some shiny, others dull. They will experience through their senses rough barnacles on wind breaks, hard stones on their feet and then warm dry sand, cold wet sand and icy cold sea round their ankles and on their bodies. They will discover the ease of taking a pushchair down a slope to the beach and the difficulty of pushing it across sand and pebbles, feel the force of the wind and the intense heat of the sun, and put on or remove clothes accordingly. They will watch ice cream melt and listen to sounds nearby and in the distance – a ship's siren, screeching seagulls or children playing in the sea. Their sense of smell will be excited by the salt sea, dead shellfish, seaweed, fish and chips and sun lotion. The daily cycle of sun rising and setting and mid-day heat along with changing tides will give a pattern to the day and indicate passing time.

Building techniques will be refined as sand castles are strengthened and children learn about the best tools for the job. They will be learning about a different environment as they see the sea and sky meeting on the horizon and notice distinctive buildings such as beach huts, the pier and amusement arcades. Rhythm will be all around as waves crash on the sand or recede over pebbles with a regular swishing sound.

Children will rarely be still as they run, dig, carry, swim or splash in the sea and invent games. Adults may choose to play with them but they will happily continue on their own, motivated by the range of exciting experiences and sensory input. In other words, they are learning because the whole experience is active, enjoyable and child-led rather than adult-dictated.

It is difficult to translate these pictures to the world of the child or young person with profound and multiple learning difficulties (PMLD) but the illustration establishes important principles for teachers of people of all abilities and ages – look for the learning potential in every situation, provide motivating learning opportunities and appropriate means of access, and encourage an active approach to learning in order to promote understanding rather than the acquisition of a list of skills. Ideas in this book have evolved from years of experience of working with pupils with PMLD, across the age range, backed up by research at the Centre for Special Education at Westminster College. A wide audience has been envisaged during the writing period to include anyone working with, or likely to encounter children or young people for whom a sensory approach to learning is all important: trainee teachers; teachers in special schools or mainstream who are struggling to find ways of including pupils with PMLD with their peer group; teachers with years of experience of pupils with PMLD who may be feeling the need of renewed inspiration; other involved professionals; parents and carers and classroom assistants. A further audience could include playgroup and preschool leaders and nursery teachers for whom a sensory approach to teaching is equally applicable. Space does not permit detailed discussion of all the issues raised, but for those wishing to explore further there are suggestions for additional reading material in the second part of the book, together with a list of resources and addresses. It is worth pointing out that any organisations, stockists or resources suggested are those with which the author is familiar and are not necessarily recommended as being better than any others.

Taylor and Hallgarten (2000) report an educationalist as saying, 'There is a new generation of teachers who have had the content and now the method of every lesson spelt out to them. They have got used to it, they rely on it. If you were to ask those teachers to start to design their own lessons and innovate as professionals, many of them would panic'. Until recently, teachers in special schools in England have not had the opportunity to fall into this trap as they have struggled to make a curriculum devised for mainstream pupils appropriate for pupils who may never reach Level 1. The needs of these pupils are belatedly being taken into consideration, but a creative and imaginative approach to teaching and learning will always be essential. Perhaps the illustration of the seaside will inspire readers to look afresh at the opportunities provided by an active approach to learning, delivered with a sense of fun in an exciting and motivating environment.

PART 1

CHAPTER 1

Why a sensory approach?

In the chaotic world of puzzlement and powerlessness created by profound and multiple learning disability and sensory impairment, we as trusted individuals can help the learner to make sense of his or her world, pointing out significance, mediating sensations, understanding expressions, protecting from overload and enabling achievement.

(Brown *et al.* 1998 p. 35)

This quote must summarise the difficulties faced by children with profound and multiple learning difficulties and the aims of those who work or live with them and whose concern is to enable them to have the very highest quality of life possible. Six major types of sensory input to the brain must be considered when planning a sensory approach to teaching: visual; auditory; kinaesthetic (the body-image component); tactile; olfactory and gustatory. Involving all the senses in the learning process may be the only way these children will be able to make sense of the world, and the aim of this book is to explore the possibilities of presenting the curriculum in such a way to pupils with complex needs.

Over the years, Piaget's theory of child development has had a powerful influence on thinking. Barber (1994) identifies the two main premises of his theory with particular implications for the cognitive development of pupils with PMLD. The first is that development is the result of complex interactions between the child and his or her environment and the second is that the general sequence of development is both universal and invariant. This does not mean that there will necessarily be a straight progression from one stage to the next for pupils with complex needs, but knowledge of normal development is essential if we are to understand their learning needs and help them to move on.

As soon as they are born, children with any sensory impairment are at a disadvantage. Piaget (1952) explores the pattern of normal development in the sensori-motor stages of babies from birth to two years of age. He describes the first stage as the 'primary circular motion' when an infant's movements are involuntary and do not seem to have any link with outside events. Examples of such actions are hand watching and random kicking or hitting strung rattles. He observes that things change at around three months, when babies seem to notice that their actions can effect their environment and they become more deliberate, for example mobiles make interesting noises and shapes when hit or kicked. At this stage of 'secondary circular reactions' infants start to show an understanding and an anticipation of the results of their movements and this awareness of cause and effect is considered to be the foundation on which all subsequent learning develops. This assumes, however, that babies are receiving feedback from their actions in the form of interesting sights, sounds or feels and that they are able to organise their bodies sufficiently well to repeat the action. For children with sensory impairment and additional physical disability this will not be possible.

Of equal significance is the probable loss of social interactions experienced by babies with PMLD from the earliest stage. Where there is multisensory impairment they will be unable to pick up on facial expressions, gestures or tone of voice and their own expressions may be equally difficult to interpret. Parents may become discouraged and without the reward of meaningful feedback in the form of a smile, noises or body movement they may interact less and less with their babies and make their own interpretation of their needs. Infants will retreat into their own world and become powerless and vulnerable. In order to compensate for this sense of isolation and confusion they may indulge in self-stimulating and stereotyped behaviour such as head banging, rocking, eye poking or aggression. If such behaviour becomes obsessive, children will become even less responsive to their environment or people in it and increasingly reluctant to use the senses they do have to explore and widen their experiences.

Young babies would normally receive sensory input from their surroundings and also from within their own body system. Brown *et al.* (1998) describe the first as external sensory input received from a distance, such as light reflected from an object, providing information relating to shape, size, colour etc. The second is described as internal sensory input received from within the body system from the senses of touch, taste and smell, providing information about the body's position in space. They say that when distance senses are impaired, the immediate environment increases in significance. Once again the child may retreat into himself and indulge in stereotypic behaviour in order to escape from a world that seems to be chaotic, unreliable and a possible threat, or alternatively may over-react to stimuli and become highly distractable. It may seem desirable to bombard a passive child with sensory experiences but Brown *et al.* argue that this could result in increased confusion. They suggest that a lively classroom may not be the optimal learning environment for someone with impairment of the distance senses and that there will need to be careful organisation in the way activities are presented. The important task of the staff will be to structure the physical and social environment in such a way as to promote an understanding of the world which is safe, consistent, interactive, fun and responsive to the learner.

Aitken and Buultjens (1992 p. 1) quote evidence of visual impairment in 50 per cent of children with cerebral palsy, as there is a close association between the development of the eye and the brain. They say that, unfortunately, these visual disorders often go unrecognised as widely available tests of visual functioning usually expect a certain level of cognitive ability, understanding or use of language. They have produced a manual with pages that can be freely photocopied to test what learners actually *do* see, how they use the vision and other senses they have, and ideas for developing a curriculum for each of the senses and at a level appropriate for the child. All the tests can be carried out without the help of experts but they would necessarily be time consuming and an extra pair of hands would be needed in the classroom. For anyone who is serious about helping children with multiple disabilities to make the most of the abilities they do possess, such testing would build up a very good picture of the 'whole' child and establish a baseline from which to build an individual learning programme, although it is strongly advised that a speech and language therapist is consulted throughout the planning process. Other assessment schedules for non-verbal children are listed below under Suggested further reading.

Ouvry (1991) identifies the foundation skills for learning as 'the ability to focus; sustain attention; filter out competing stimuli and interact purposefully with both people and objects'. These will be skills that most of our pupils will be working on throughout their lives, but this does not necessitate a boring repetition of experiences or childish activities. Although the emphasis is on a sensory approach to the curriculum for pupils with PMLD, this approach to learning is important for everyone, and it would be encouraging to think that practice in special schools could influence teaching methods in mainstream classrooms. Most of us respond to environments that are planned to sooth the senses, as was observed by watching people of all ages sitting or lying in 'Rest', the relaxation area of the Dome in Greenwich, London. To quote Madina (1999 p. 41) in the *Millennium Experience*:

> Entering through a hidden, sound absorbing approach, we step inside to experience deep calm. Rest creates a sense of peace by appealing to our senses. In this zone with no edges, no beginning and no end, beautiful layers of light and colour slowly wash against the sky. Gently evolving music loops through cadences at changing pitches and speeds.

For more proof of the need of all human beings to experience the world through their senses, observe adults in any big department store. From the moment of entering they may experience warm air, soothing music, soft pile carpet under their feet and distinctive smells. Colours are compared, materials are felt and cosmetics smelt – shopping over the Internet can never be a substitute for such a total sensory experience, for as John Keats said in a letter to Fanny Brawne (8 July 1819), 'Nothing ever becomes real til it is experienced'. Longhorn (1996/7) identifies at least 26 senses which we use all our lives and says that encouraging children to use their senses will permeate every aspect of their learning and stay with them for ever. If we are aiming to educate children for life, this must surely be one of the best reasons for advocating a sensory approach to learning for everyone regardless of physical or mental ability.

Suggested further reading

Glenn, S. M. (1988) 'Activities to encourage children's development in the early years', in Smith, B. (ed.) *Interactive Approaches to the Education of Children with Severe Learning Difficulties*. Birmingham: Westhill College.

Longhorn, F. (1993) – see Bibliography.

Ouvry, C. (1987) *Educating children with profound handicaps*. Worcs: BIMH Publications.

Ouvry, C. and Saunders, S. (1996) – see Bibliography.

Literature and educational videos may be obtained from The Royal National Institute for the Blind, 224 Great Portland Street, London WIW 5AA. Tel: 020 7388 1266.

For assessment scales based on Piaget's theory of child development, see:

Hogg, J. and Sebba, J. (1986) *Profound Retardation and Multiple Impairment, vols. 1 and 2*. London: Croom Helm.

Hogg, J. and Raines, N. (eds) (1987) *Assessment in Mental Handicap*. London: Croom Helm.

For assessment schedules see the suggested further reading for Chapter 10.

CHAPTER 2

Developing a sensory approach to the curriculum

In my view, just talking about children knowing, understanding and doing leaves out the major curriculum goal, which is to help children learn what they need to learn, to know what they need to know, and to be able to do certainly what they need to be able to do.

(Katz 2000)

What is a sensory curriculum?

It is important to put in context the development of the curriculum documents in Part 2 of this book because important principles have been established during the process. The starting point was the invitation to work with a special school for pupils with physical disabilities and a range of learning difficulties in the development of a 'sensory curriculum'. In order to establish exactly what was needed we looked at three different attitudes to the position of a sensory curriculum within a school and the ways in which teachers use it as identified by Ouvry and Saunders (1996, pp. 206–7):

1. It can be used to stimulate the senses with activities based on stages of sensory development and the acquisition of basic skills identified as priorities in the pupil's Individual Education Programmes (IEPs).
2. It can be incorporated into activities which have their own structure and meaning such as drama, music and massage.
3. It can be used as an access route to subject-based activities.

The first position suggests a separate sensory curriculum and, while there is a place for providing structured activities for helping pupils to acquire the basic skills as identified by Ouvry (1991) and noted in the previous chapter, it was agreed that the ultimate aim must be an increased understanding of the environment and the wider world. Figure 2.1 illustrates how this can work in practice where skills taught in a controlled environment are practised in an extended range of situations with pupils returning regularly to reinforce skills and learn new ones. There was agreement about the third position, as teachers acknowledged that a sensory approach is the *only* access route to subject-based activities for most pupils with PMLD. However, if it is accepted that pupils are to be given the opportunity to access the same curriculum as the rest of the school population, few activities should need their own structure and meaning as most learning outcomes can be encompassed within the existing subjects. It was eventually concluded that teachers were asking for ideas and resources for presenting the curriculum to pupils for whom it was not appropriate in its present form – in other words, what they were requesting was *a sensory approach to the curriculum* and not *a sensory curriculum* – a subtle but important difference.

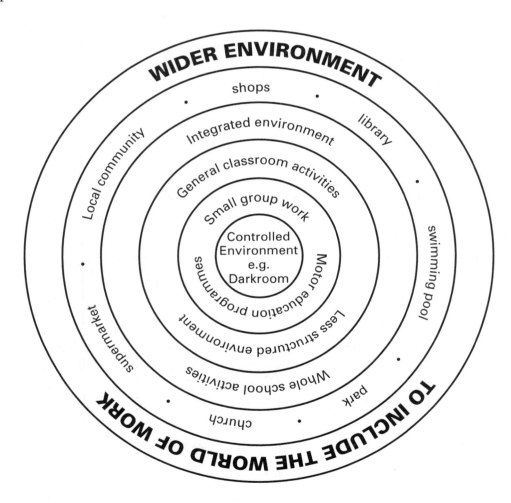

Figure 2.1 This diagram describes a continuous learning process, where skills taught in a controlled environment are practised in a widening range of environments

Planning under subjects

The School Curriculum and Assessment Authority (SCAA 1996 p. 12) was the first national document to suggest that pupils with PMLD could benefit from a subject based approach to learning, saying that 'subject specific contexts can be provided to teach skills identified in a pupil's individuals targets, whether they are directly related to the subject or not'. The National Literacy Strategy (DfEE 1998) and the National Numeracy Strategy (DfEE 1999) have certainly helped to clarify the teaching and learning involved within these subjects, but there may still be a need for specialist training if staff are to be clear about the skills and areas of knowledge and understanding across the range of subjects. Grove and Peacey (1999 p. 85) discuss problems which can arise when trying to deliver a subject-based curriculum for pupils operating at early developmental levels, and say that the theoretical rationale for this has never been addressed. They discuss the various strategies adopted by schools and conclude that it is vital to be clear about the nature of the learning task and to identify the learning which must be involved within a subject, namely:

- exposure to experiences that are critical to that subject or domain;
- a grasp of the knowledge base that is particular to that subject or domain;
- developing ways of understanding the world that are characteristic of that subject or domain.

The DES (1989 4.3) acknowledges, however, the cross-curricular aspects of learning at an early stage of development and suggests that 'the use of subjects to define the National Curriculum does not mean that teaching has to be organised and delivered within prescribed boundaries'. Cross-curricular themes and activities are recommended as being particularly appropriate for pupils for whom the processes of learning are similar within a variety of activities. From experience, whole-school planning round a topic or module offers opportunities for shared ideas, pooled resources and real inclusion for pupils with PMLD with their peer group. It is important to remember, however, that cross-curricular delivery of the curriculum still necessitates good knowledge of the learning outcomes for individual subjects. Further reading on this subject can be found in the final section of this chapter.

Developing a broad and balanced curriculum

It was decided to use Level 1 of the mainstream curriculum as an 'umbrella' for planning, but at the same time nobody wanted to stress curriculum coverage at the expense of the particular learning needs of the pupils. QCA (1999 p. 5) identifies learning aims for schools to use when developing their own curriculum These provided useful guidelines for drawing up life skills that pupils need to work towards and achieve. Particular needs of pupils with PMLD were included and the completed list was divided between four life areas. Links with subjects were explored (see DfE 1995, and DfEE/QCA 1999) and it soon became obvious that there is a close relationship between national curriculum subjects at all key stages and the key skills. This is particularly evident at an early developmental level as has been acknowledged in the recent curriculum guidelines for pupils attaining significantly below age-related expectations. At the time of writing these are at the consultation stage, and the level descriptions P1(a)–P3(b) are generic across the scales, but in order to simplify the procedure it was decided to link the learning needs with subjects according to their *particular* contribution to the school curriculum (QCA 1999 and DfEE 1999). Each stage of this process is demonstrated in Figure 2.2.

The conclusion at this point was that the National Curriculum is able to offer a good basis for planning a broad and balanced curriculum for pupils with PMLD, with necessary adaptations to ensure appropriate access to learning objectives. However, attempting to teach and record under all the subject headings could be complicated and unrealistic. The previous exercise had revealed that the core subjects (highlighted on Figure 2.2) cover most skills at an early stage of learning, and activities and strategies for teaching these subjects can cover the themes and dimensions of subjects across the curriculum, as illustrated by the example in Figure 2.3.

In the light of research and findings, the decision was made to restrict planning to the core subjects initially. Attainment Targets (ATs) at Level 1 set the learning objectives, and programmes of study, with accompanying suggested activities and resources, were devised for working towards these objectives. The resulting curriculum document can be found in Part 2 of this book and issues surrounding recording and assessing are discussed further in Chapter 10.

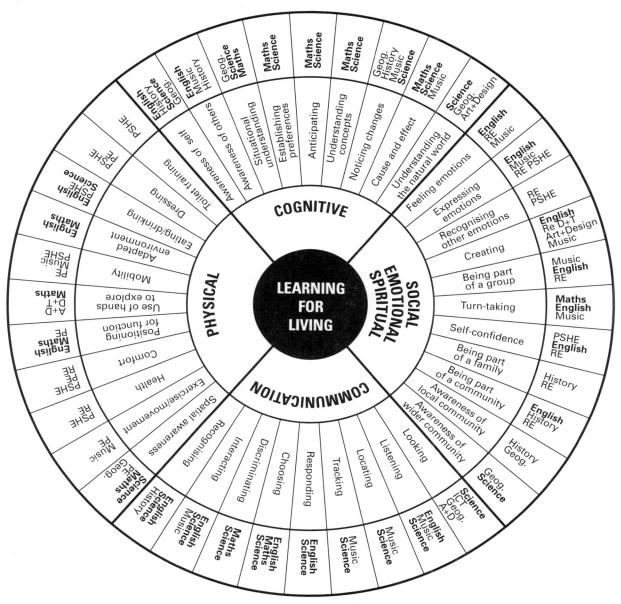

Stage 1: Identified learning aims and particular needs of pupils with PMLD

Stage 2: Learning aims divided between four life areas

Stage 3: Links with subjects according to their distinctive contribution to the curriculum

Stage 4: Extent to which aims and needs are covered by the core subjects (highlighted)

NB ICT will be used to aid access to the curriculum and to support learning in all subjects

Figure 2.2 Developing a broad and balanced curriculum

Science: Life processes and living things			
AT 2 Level 1	**POS**	**Specific body awareness programmes**	**Curriculum coverage**
Pupils recognise and name external parts of the body, using words such as head and arm.	Encourage body awareness through involvement in a range of activities.	Physical programmes to include exercise, swimming, soft play area, hands group, music and movement with one to one support.	Music PE
		Patting and naming parts of the body (e.g. Tac Pac), aromatherapy massage.	RE English
		Self-care activities.	PSHE
		Clapping and stamping games, rhyming songs, rap rhythm.	Music English PE
		Resonance board, foot spa, vibrating equipment to touch or lie on, dark room activities.	ICT Other areas of Science
		Finger painting, body prints, collage, clay etc.	Art and Design Design and Technology

Figure 2.3 An example of how strategies for teaching a core subject involve subjects across the curriculum

Suggested further reading

Whole curriculum planning

Byers, R. and Rose, R. (1995) *Planning the Curriculum for Pupils with Special Educational Needs: A Practical Guide.* London: David Fulton Publishers.

Longhorn, F. (1993a) – see Bibliography

Longhorn F. (1995) – see Bibliography.

Rose, R. *et al.* (1996) *Implementing the Whole Curriculum for Pupils with Learning Difficulties.* London: David Fulton Publishers.

Sebba, J. *et al.* (1993) *Redefining the Whole Curriculum for Pupils with Learning Difficulties.* London: David Fulton Publishers.

Subject planning

The 'Entitlement for All' series by David Fulton Publishers covers numerous subjects including: reading; writing; physical education; religious education; art; music; information technology; geography; history; science; mathematics and dance.

Other useful titles are:

Richards, R. *et al.* (1995) *An Early Start to Science.* Cheltenham: Stanley Thornes.

The following publications by Flo Longhorn are available from Catalyst Education Resources (see contact details under Suppliers and useful addresses in the Resources Section, Part 2).

Longhorn, F. (1993b) – see Bibliography.

Longhorn, F. (1997) *Sex Education and Sexuality for Very Special People – A Sensory Approach.* Wootton, Beds: Catalyst Education Resources.

Longhorn, F. (1997b) – see Bibliography.

Longhorn, F. (2000) *Numeracy for Very Special Learners: Resource Pack.* Wootton, Beds: Catalyst Education Resources.

Longhorn, F. (2000) *Sensory Drama for Very Special Learners.* Wootton, Beds: Catalyst Education Resources.

CHAPTER 3

When to deliver the curriculum

Longhorn describes a sensory approach to the curriculum as happening at 'any place, any time, anywhere' (1993 p. 7).

Fagg *et al.* (1990 pp. 23–4) while discussing the delivery of a broad, balanced and relevant curriculum, describe three aspects that need to be taken into consideration. These are:

- the core curriculum, covering essential areas of learning;
- the open curriculum, which is all educational opportunities not considered absolutely essential; and
- the hidden curriculum, which involves many undocumented aspects of school life.

For pupils with physical and health problems, the curriculum will necessarily have to include aspects which would not be considered essential for the majority of students in mainstream, and the hidden curriculum will also be an integral part of their school day. Pupils who feel unwell or uncomfortable will be unable to learn and therefore their physical well-being *must* be a first priority. The teacher will be responsible for consulting with the relevant professionals as to the correct furniture and positioning for individual pupils in order to ensure that they have optimum hand and body function and for advice on personal feeding programmes and exercise programmes tailored to the needs of each child. Allowance will also need to be made for the time it takes to move pupils from one position to another several times a day and to deal with health issues that may arise. Lewis (1995 p. 27) suggests that teachers of primary aged children can help to fit the NC into a tight school day by following the principle of 'any place, any time, anywhere'. She cites an example of using the time on a bus journey to the swimming pool to develop the children's observation of the area and to practise rhymes and singing games. How much more will the teacher of pupils with PMLD, with a large proportion of the day taken up with physical needs, have to use an imaginative and flexible approach to the delivery of the curriculum.

When there is good knowledge of individual pupils and their learning needs, coupled with good knowledge of the curriculum, a teacher will be aware of all contexts throughout the day as offering opportunities for sensory learning. All staff, including those working with children outside the classroom, need to be included in the process of looking for individual pupil's reactions and achievements and as far as possible should be included in discussions about Individual Education Plans (IEPs). When Programmes of Study (PoS) are linked to learning goals there will be good understanding of the reasons behind activities and this will be discussed further in Chapter 10.

While accepting that many of the things which pupils with PMLD do throughout the day are not obviously educational, every activity has the potential for teaching and learning and these activities should be planned and recorded as carefully as more formal teaching sessions. It is enlightening to realise how many areas of the curriculum can be involved in everyday activities, for example dressing and undressing or going to the bathroom. It is worth carrying out useful exercises such as those demonstrated in Figures 3.1 and 3.2 to prove the possibilities for teaching and learning in what could otherwise be seen as wasted time.

Pupils with a physical disability will need regular exercise to prevent deterioration and to keep them comfortable. Most activities will provide opportunities for some exercise and correct positioning, but there will also be the need for specific exercise programmes. If these take place in the morning this may be the time of day when pupils are most receptive and the only time when they will have one to one attention from an adult. If adults have good knowledge of the children they are working with and understand their physical and learning needs, these sessions will be great teaching opportunities. The example in Figure 3.3 demonstrates how one aspect of the topic for the term was delivered in a physical programme, with the added advantage of keeping both adults and children awake and interested through what could have been yet another set of boring exercises!

Suggested further reading

All the works cited in this chapter are recommended reading. Full details are in the Bibliography.

Sensory experience	Learning opportunities Pupils should be able to:
Smell Bodily smells – nice and nasty Air freshener Soap Talcum powder Toothpaste	Indicate an understanding of the environment through the use of sensory clues (refer to Level Descriptions on sample recording sheet in Part 2 to assess level of response).
Feel Toothbrush, hairbrush Toothmug Flannel and towel Soap Hot and cold water Vibration of electric toothbrush Body movement (up and down in hoist) (Put tactile initials on belongings where appropriate)	Make a link between tactile initial letter of first name and themselves. Show awareness of similarities in properties of objects and materials e.g. all brushes, all towelling. Show awareness of contrasts such as: rough/smooth, wet/dry, hot/cold. Use a switch (on the electric toothbrush) to cause a change in movement.
Taste Toothpaste – use different flavours	Develop skills of sucking, licking, lip closure.
Look at Self in mirror Others in mirror Face while washing Face while cleaning teeth Symbols to indicate objects and activities in the bathroom e.g. toilet, taps, washing, teeth cleaning, bath	Indicate awareness of self. Indicate awareness of others. Show an awareness of body parts. Make a link between object and symbol.
Listen to Running water (turn tap/push lever) Splashing Teeth being brushed Hair being brushed Toilet flushing (pull chain/push handle) Language to indicate body parts, positions, change of activity	Locate sounds. Track sounds. Indicate an understanding of the environment through auditory clues. Cause changes through pushing and pulling actions.

Figure 3.1 Delivering the curriculum through regular, routine activities – Using the bathroom

Activity	Learning opportunity Pupils should be able to:
Greet on arrival. Sign and say 'Hello' and pupil's name.	Indicate an awareness of self. Respond to own name. Indicate an awareness of others. Interact with others. Make a link between the initial of their name and themselves.
Unpack bags together.	When handling objects, show an awareness in differences in shape, size or weight.
Remove outdoor clothing, giving pupils as much independence as possible.	Show an awareness of body parts. Relate objects to their proper functions.
Take clothes and bags to hang on own peg (fix photo of pupil by peg).	Recognise photo of self.
Find their own clothes at the end of the day. Show two coats or two bags etc. Allow pupils to feel the textures of materials and give time for them to indicate recognition of their own possessions.	Show awareness of similarities in properties of objects and materials e.g. both coats or both bags. Show awareness of contrasts such as rough/smooth. Recognise own belongings.
Dress to go home. Pull clothes and bag off peg. Push arms into coats. Count fingers into gloves.	Cause changes by pushing and pulling actions. Develop an awareness of rote counting.
NB Keeping to a routine for everyday activities will enable pupils to use cues to build up a picture of the environment, anticipate the next event and understand the order of the day.	

Figure 3.2 Delivering the curriculum through regular, routine activities – Beginning and ending of the school day: dressing and undressing

Positioning/Skills	Activity	Resources
Pupils sitting on stools holding onto ladders, adults behind to give support as necessary Holding on with two hands Bottoms back Feet flat Head up Standing practice where appropriate Grasp and release Holding with one hand while using the other	Greet each pupil in turn and wait for response. Leader slowly turns rain stick or ocean drum to make 'rainy' sounds. Sound gets louder. Hand round umbrellas – pupils release bar with one hand and hold umbrella. Spray umbrellas and hands lightly with water. Sing 'rainy' songs. Release umbrellas and hold on with two hands.	Stools Ladders or ladder-back chairs Mats Arm and leg gaiters Rain sticks Ocean drum Small umbrella for each pupil Towels 'Rain' songs or poems e.g. 'It's raining, it's pouring' 'I'm singing in the rain'
Move to long-sitting on mats with adult support from behind (use arm and leg gaiters where necessary) Balance in sitting Use of hand and fingers Rotation of wrists	Take round percussion instruments, trays of rice or lentils, rain sticks etc. – each pupil to use hands and fingers to make 'rainy' sounds in turn. Listen to each other's sounds – locate in turn.	Percussion instruments Materials which make a 'tinkly' sound Tin trays Rain sticks to turn Light and mirror ball for raindrop effect

Figure 3.3 Topic for the term: Sound.
Theme for this lesson: Weather Sounds

CHAPTER 4

How to deliver the curriculum

A focused approach

Pupils with a fragmented view of the world will need time to learn to look and listen in a distraction-free environment for parts of the day. These areas can be specially equipped dark or light rooms or an adapted area of the classroom. The Resources section in Part 2 has suggestions for toys and other materials to encourage children to look and locate in a darkened room, and the Curriculum document in Part 2 has ideas for suitable activities. There is an example in Chapter 9 of using a simple drama session in a dark room to encourage looking and listening skills, and once teachers start to experiment themselves they will be excited by the possibilities. Longhorn (1997a) suggests ways of using ultraviolet light to reinforce the curriculum and, whether or not this is available, activities can be adapted for use with alternative light sources, even as simple as a torch. Expensive equipment is not necessary – of greatest importance is the imagination and enthusiasm of the teacher and his or her relationship with the pupils. Skills learned in these settings will need to be practised in small groups in the classroom, in larger, whole school activities and in the wider community. Pupils may need to return to a controlled environment regularly throughout their lives, but the emphasis should always be on offering opportunities to use a sensory approach to learning in contexts which mirror real life as closely as possible (see Figure 2.1).

A 'fun' approach

For many teachers the discovery of a sensory approach to teaching came as a breath of fresh air after the rigid and restricted behavioural programmes they had been using. At last it was realised that teaching could be fun and pupils could be actively involved in their own learning. The importance of play cannot be underestimated and as Denziloe (1994 p. 9) says, 'we ought to develop our play from womb to tomb'. For babies and young children there is no distinction between work and play and toddlers will move things in and out of containers for sheer enjoyment, unaware of the fact that they are learning through these activities. For children with little movement or control over their limbs, the idea of play is a difficult one. We automatically associate play with toys, but this is probably the most difficult aspect for our pupils. It is up to the adults who live and work with them to provide the materials, environment and social situations to encourage attitudes of curiosity and the chance to enjoy learning.

The Resource section in Part 2 lists individuals and organisations that work on the principle of learning through fun and interactive activities. Many of these use pupils' enjoyment of sound and rhythm as a starting point, and Chapter 9 explores the possibilities of extending activities into the realm of drama. In an atmosphere of enjoyment and mutual trust children will develop a sound self-image and an understanding of themselves in relation to others. Bentley (2000 p. 19) says that 'trust – secure, trusting relationships are vital to environments in which people are prepared to take risks, and can learn from failure'. That statement is as applicable to adults working with pupils as it is to the pupils themselves. Creative ideas will flourish when people feel free to experiment.

'Fun' materials

Galileo (1564–1642) said 'You cannot teach a man anything, you can only help him discover it for himself'. All children must be given opportunities to investigate, problem solve and interpret what is happening, but for pupils with severe physical and learning difficulties the motivating factors to do so will need to be stronger than the obstacles raised. When choosing toys, equipment or materials to offer to pupils, Ouvry and Mitchell (1995 p. 190), suggest we ask ourselves: 'what the person will find most interesting; which will offer the most opportunity for the practice and integration of current skills; which will develop new skills most effectively and which will provide the greatest sense of pleasure and achievement'.

Before we can answer these questions we need to understand the likes and dislikes of individual pupils, what motivates them to want to explore, their means of communicating what they enjoy doing and how they indicate a choice of activity. First of all they must be given the opportunity to play and explore on their own in positions allowing for maximum function. A range of materials and toys should be offered and all reactions should be recorded in as much detail as possible. From experience, the use of a video camera is invaluable and provides the opportunity to pick up on small communications which may otherwise be missed. For some pupils it may be necessary to carry out a formal assessment and the Resources section in Part 2 offers suggestions for these. We must never forget that parents, grandparents and carers are the experts on their own children and should be consulted at every stage.

Once we have decided on aspects of playthings which the pupil finds most attractive, such as shiny surfaces, noise-making toys and materials, music-making equipment etc. we can decide what to buy or make. It is a mistake to think that expensive, specialised equipment will be best. Nowadays there are plenty of exciting and inexpensive things in the shops and catalogues delivered through our doors, and it is well worth exploring these first. The resource section at the back of the book has information about stockists and suggests books with imaginative ideas for those who are willing to spend a little time to make their own resources. An added advantage of buying or making economical playthings is that they can be used in a versatile way and can be discarded when worn out or when pupils need to be encouraged to move on to practise new skills.

A 'fun' environment

What is a fun environment for one child may be a nightmare for another. One child may love noise and boisterous activity and another may like peace and quiet. While pupils will benefit from being exposed to a range of experiences, this will need to be a gradual process and we should never force unpleasant situations on anyone. If play is to be enjoyable there must be the opportunity for choice, and once again it will be important to identify means of expressing likes and dislikes and then to respect those choices. It is worth looking at the possibilities for having fun with others in the community, as the more real and 'normal' the situation the better. Possibilities include local swimming pools, jacuzzis, sensory gardens, ball pools and soft-play areas, zoos, the seaside, greenhouses in botanical gardens, 'rainforests', the cinema, circus, concert hall, theatre and ice-skating rinks.

In recent years more attention has been paid to the quality of life of people with multiple disabilities, and specialised environments have been designed with their particular needs in mind. The best example of these is the 'snoezelen' or multi-sensory environment. The 'snoezelen' was originally developed in the Netherlands at the Hartenberg Institute in order to extend the range of leisure opportunities for their residents who were becoming increasingly disabled. The idea was to provide a place for gentle stimulation and relaxation where there was no pressure to achieve or learn skills.

'Snoezelen' was introduced into the United Kingdom by Rompa and this type of environment has now become very popular and can be found in special schools and many institutions. For information about multisensory rooms, ways in which they can be used and where to buy equipment, see the Resources section in Part 2, and for ideas for inexpensive ways of 'doing it yourself' see Denziloe (1994 p. 70–2).

However we decide to use these rooms, we should not forget that they were originally developed in order to bring pleasure and relaxation to people for whom life was not much fun. The basic system can be developed and switching devices introduced to give pupils some control over the effects produced, but enjoyment should be the motivating factor, not outside pressure to achieve. Nor should these environments ever be seen as convenient places to leave pupils for some form of sensory stimulation while the staff have a break – it is important for adults and pupils to enjoy themselves together. From experience these can be times of real communication and bonding and a good opportunity for working one to one with pupils with calming activities such as hand and foot massage.

An interactive approach

Changes in attitude in education have filtered through to special schools and the move towards integration for pupils with special needs has made it even more imperative to keep in tune with mainstream philosophy. Emphasis has changed from a teacher-led approach to a pupil-led approach, with pupils having input into their records of achievement and into setting their own learning targets. For teachers of pupils with severe learning difficulties this has involved exploring ways of handing control over to pupils as opposed to the old reliance on behavioural theories and structured programmes for the training of skills. The philosophy behind this approach is that of creating a responsive environment in which adults are encouraged to follow the pupil's lead, assume attempts to communicate and respond appropriately. Motivating factors will be identified and these will form the basis for teaching and learning, and eventually contact with peers and participation in the curriculum can be possible for pupils who had previously been isolated. Collis and Lacey (1996) say that teachers need to have a clear understanding of the process rather than a preoccupation with the end to be reached and that under-standing is the important aim rather than the acquisition of skills. The quality of relationship between adult and pupil is all-important in this approach and adults must be sensitive to feedback from the learner and have respect for their attempts to communicate. Aherne and Thornber (1990) describe a process of encouraging communication in pupils with little or no speech. They use playful activities between adult and child as opportunities for keeping detailed observation of responses, and suggest ways of helping pupils to progress from a prescriptive to an interactive approach to learning. For those wanting to know more about an interactive approach to learning there is a list of titles in the Suggested further reading section, below. The following example from an activity in a Beat That! session demonstrates this way of working in practice with the adult taking the lead from the pupil by picking up on a particular movement or sound, mirroring it, augmenting it and using it to make a rhythmical pattern which can be shared by the group. Using this approach, pupils are encouraged to realise that they *can* have control and eventually their actions will become more deliberate and meaningful.

Example

People involved are two pupils, a leader and a helper. One pupil is lying on the resonance board and the other (Dan) has crawled to the edge of the room.

Dan obviously listening and interested, but reluctant to join in.
Leader watches Dan's movements and mirrors them.
Dan starts to clap. Leader claps in rhythm and then bangs on the board and calls his name.
Dan crawls to the board puts his hands on the board and taps. He puts his helper's hand on the board.
Dan's tapping becomes rhythmical and the leader keeps time with him.
The leader bangs on the board and counts.
Dan becomes excited and moves to sit on the edge of the board.
Dan claps again and the leader repeats his rhythm.
Dan puts his hands up in the air, bangs them down on the board and scrapes the board. This sequence is repeated several times.
The leader repeats his sequence and Dan puts his ear on the board to listen.

A holistic approach

It is very easy for professionals working with pupils with complex needs to be looking at their particular 'part' of the child instead of seeing them as a whole person. Difficulties arise for the teacher when a pupil is frequently removed from the classroom for individual therapy sessions or when furniture is provided, without consultation, which subsequently proves unsuitable for use in group settings or with classroom furniture. Other professionals wince when they see children working in uncomfortable positions or being fed in an insensitive manner. Among points raised at the Special Educational Needs conferences in March 1999 and reported in QCA/DfEE (1999) was the need for improved multi-agency cooperation. New proposed funding flexibility between the National Health Service and local authorities was welcomed, but it was recognised that other barriers still remained such as different priorities and a lack of common terminology. Ideally there should be the opportunity for all members of the team working with the pupils to plan and discuss together and to pass on their particular area of knowledge. Without this co-operation pupils will not receive consistent and integrated care and education. With careful organisation teachers and therapists can plan and work together to deliver the curriculum and it should not be necessary to withdraw pupils for individual programmes.

An age-appropriate approach

There is a danger that we can become too concerned with providing pupils with age-appropriate play materials and thus deny them the basic right of enjoyment and the opportunity to practise new skills. Pupils with PMLD will enjoy the sort of games enjoyed between mothers and babies and they should be allowed to experience emotional fulfilment and social contact through such playful activities. Collis and Lacey (1996 p. 20) say that 'age-appropriateness need not be a problem if it is more related to respect for individuals and enabling them to take some control over their own lives than to whether teenagers and adults should indulge in childish activities'. Denziloe (1994) also comments that it is sometimes the activity which is inappropriate and not the equipment. An illustration will help to demonstrate these points:

Example

David was 14 years old and for a whole year his teacher had been working to persuade him to hand over a named object or put a variety of objects in and out of a box – all to no avail. One day, in a group hand exercise class, another teacher asked him to pass round the sticks and to her surprise he did so immediately. At the end of the session she asked him to collect up the sticks and put them back in the box. Once again he obliged straight away and from then on nobody else was allowed to take the job away from him. Once he could see the purpose of the activity he had pride in his achievement and for the first time was able to enjoy taking responsibility. From then on there was no holding him back and he was soon manipulating his wheelchair for the first time and had taken over the task of delivering the class register to the office.

For pupils with PMLD, aged 14-16 and beyond, there are at least two schemes offering approved accreditation awards and appropriate working environments for older pupils to demonstrate the skills they have been practising. These schemes are discussed further in Chapter 10 and contact information can be found in the Supplier addresses section in Part 2.

Suggested further reading

A 'fun' approach

See the reading material in the Play and Leisure section under Resources (Part 2). The Winslow catalogue (Tel: 01869 244644) lists books on play therapy.

A structured approach

Longhorn, F. (1997a) – see Bibliography.

An interactive approach to teaching

Byers, R. (1994) 'Providing Opportunities for Effective Learning' in Rose, R. *et al.* (eds) *Implementing the Whole Curriculum for Pupils with Learning Difficulties.* London: David Fulton Publishers.

Collis, M. and Lacey, P. (1996) – see Bibliography.

Grove, N. and Park, K. (1996) – see Bibliography.

Hewett, D. and Nind, M. (1998) *Interaction in Action: Reflections on the Use of Intensive Interaction.* London: David Fulton Publishers.

McConkey, R. (1981) 'Education Without Understanding?', *Special Education: Forward Trends,* **8**(3), 8–10.

Nind, M. and Hewett, D. (1988) 'Interaction as Curriculum', *British Journal of Special Education* **15**(2), 55–7.

Nind, M. and Hewett, D. (1994) *Access to Communication: Developing the Basics of Communication with People with Severe Learning Difficulties through Intensive Interaction.* London: David Fulton Publishers.

Ware (1994) (ed.) *Educating Children with Profound and Multiple Learning Difficulties.* London: David Fulton Publishers.

Ware, J. (1996) – see Bibliography.

Watson, J. (1994) 'Classroom Organisation', in Ware, J. (ed.) *Educating Children with Profound and Multiple Learning Difficulties.* London: David Fulton Publishers.

A holistic approach

Coles, C. (1994) 'A Multi-Disciplinary Approach to the Whole Curriculum', in Rose, R. *et al.* (eds) *Implementing the Whole Curriculum for Pupils with Learning Difficulties.* London: David Fulton Publishers.

An age-appropriate approach

Griffiths, M. (1994) *Transition to Adulthood: The Role of Education for Young People with Severe Learning Difficulties.* London: David Fulton Publishers.

Griffiths, M. and Tennyson, C. (1997) *The Extended Curriculum: Meeting the Needs of Young People.* London: David Fulton Publishers.

CHAPTER 5

Where to deliver the curriculum

If a truly balanced curriculum is to be offered by schools, the whole child in their setting at school, home and in the community must be considered.

(Fagg *et al.* 1990 p. 31)

In school

At the turn of the century the establishment of special schools was an attempt to make being in school worthwhile for those pupils who would not benefit from instruction in a general classroom. Gerber (1995) notes that special education was the beginning of inclusion, not exclusion and that it has always had the same goal. Over the past decade, however, there have been great changes for pupils in special schools. As the climate of opinion has changed, pupils with learning difficulties have been gradually integrated into mainstream education with their peer group. The implications of this are great for pupils with PMLD and their teachers, and it is important to ensure that integration for these pupils is not in name only.

It is probably unrealistic to expect relationships to develop naturally between mainstream pupils and pupils with limited means of communication and it is up to the staff working with pupils with PMLD to present them in the best possible light. Integration projects such as those described in Chapter 6 are an excellent starting point for building understanding and breaking down barriers, as pupils work together on projects that are enjoyable for everybody. Many issues surrounding the subject of 'inclusion' are aired in these case studies. Ouvry (1998) gives suggestions for providing opportunities and support for pupils with PMLD to build enriching social contacts. When staff are prepared to plan carefully in this way, integration with their mainstream peers will give pupils with PMLD dignity and improve their quality of life, while ensuring that their needs continue to be met.

At home

The future role of parent partnership services was discussed at the regional Special Educational Needs conferences in 1999. There was support for extending parent partnership services across the country, and for training for teachers, Local Education Authority officers and educational psychologists in communicating with parents. The importance of including parents at each stage of the planning process has already been mentioned, but this will only happen when there is an attitude of trust and a good relationship built up over time. Ouvry (1991 pp. 58–9) identifies the need for great sensitivity and understanding from teachers in their relationships with the parents of pupils with complex needs:

> Helping parents to have appropriate expectations for their child has always required a high degree of sensitivity in order to sustain positive expectations of progress over a long period of time, whilst accepting the limitation of the child's disability.

Parents must not be allowed to lose hope, even as their children grow older and progress seems slow. The same skills may need to be practised throughout a pupil's school life, but progression can be built into the curriculum in terms of a widening range of learning environments and experiences offered (Figure 2.1). Record keeping and reporting to the parents should reflect this progression, and these issues are discussed further in Chapter 10.

Parents should feel free to visit the school at all times and the use of home–school diaries will keep lines of communication open. Carpenter (1994) emphasises the need for early intervention and support for *all* the family members, however, as it is all too easy for everything to centre around the mother and for other family members, particularly the father, to feel left out and disempowered. He says that it is important to work hard at redressing this balance as the whole family will need to pull together in the difficult task of raising a child with complex needs – ideas for involving carers and the wider family are discussed further in Chapter 10. As a demonstration of the value of school staff and parents working together there follows a study which was undertaken with the aim of interpreting the communicative behaviour of three pupils with PMLD and no speech. Each child was filmed over a period of a school term and at the end of the filming, staff in the school, adults at home and any carers were invited to take the video home and use a questionnaire with a simple tick chart to indicate how they perceived the pupil's indication of likes and dislikes, any motivations to communicate, and responses to a cross section of adults and peers. Finally, each group watched the video together to discuss and share their findings. The results for each student were summarised on charts and given to all involved (Figure 5.1).

Adult interpretation	Brian's actions and body language
'Here I am' 'Look at me'	Looking – Smiling – Vocalising – Shouting – Touching – 'Hitting'
Asking for things Saying 'yes' Wanting more	Asks for things by looking at them, vocalising, shouting, touching and hitting them. Says 'yes' by smiling and laughing.
Saying 'no' Showing displeasure – 'leave me alone'	Lack of attention and interest – withdraws. Facial expression – pulls bottom lip up. Refuses food by keeping mouth shut.
Trying to keep another's attention	Looks at – laughs – touches – vocalises. Reaches to touch or 'hit' people. Knocks things off the table.
Drawing attention to an interesting object or event	Wanting to share a joke – looks from one adult to another whilst laughing and stiffening. Swipes at objects.

Identified motivations to communicate
Presence of favourite adults. Sharing a joke. Watching darts or football on TV with the family. Requesting favourite food. Feeling uncomfortable or insecure.

NB Brian has cerebral palsy resulting in profound and multiple learning difficulties and no speech.

Figure 5.1 The result of cooperation between school and home to interpret communicative behaviour of a pupil with PMLD

The importance of a consistent approach to communication with children with complex needs has been recognised by Barnardo's in Taunton and in 1996 the Barnardo's Somerset Inclusion Project was started. Their Early Years Service has developed three posts to include a specialist speech and language therapist, a teacher and a sessional worker who work with the parents and carers of preschool children who have little or no speech. They encourage total communication by use of objects, symbols, signs and speech, facial expression and body language, eye pointing, switch systems or any combination to meet the needs of the child. In order to ensure a consistent approach, they run the Hanen Parent Programme which offers a combination of home visits and group sessions with the aim of providing parents with an understanding of how children acquire language, helping them to promote their own children's language and enabling children and adults to connect and communicate. Their work in the wider community is discussed later.

Finally, it is worth obtaining some of the good reading matter and videos available for parents, to be kept in school and loaned out. The Winslow catalogue has a good special needs reference section and details of useful reading and videos for parents from the Royal National Institute for the Blind (RNIB). Journals and Issues such as *PMLD Link* (see Resources section) could be obtained regularly and borrowed by interested parents. Other useful information could be kept in a file for parents to access, to include subjects such as: toy libraries; leisure facilities; courses; contacts for advice and stockists for equipment. The Resources Section in part 2 of this book has relevant information for such a file.

In the community

All pupils need to extend learning contexts into the wider community but it is particularly important for older pupils to have adult situations in which to practise skills. Pupils will have been learning about using a switch to make a toy work or start the washing machine or food mixer, and learning opportunities can then be extended as they practise pressing a switch to change traffic lights or to call a lift. Similarly, their knowledge of signs can involve road and social signs and recognising the pictures of vegetables on the weighing scales in some supermarkets. For pupils at the top end of the school, accreditation schemes such as those mentioned in Chapter 10 offer programmes to extend the learning environment into the community and to ease the transition from school to college.

During the 1980s and 1990s, Barnardo's school in Taunton saw more and more of their pupils moving into mainstream provision. As these pupils moved from the sheltered environment of school into the community, there was a perceived need for a consistent system of communication, understood by the society in which they were functioning. The Barnardo's Somerset Inclusion Project, as described earlier, spread the net wider to encourage the use of total communication in playgroups, schools and playschemes. They also run a Together Project for Leisure and Recreation, which supports and encourages leisure activity providers to include disabled children and young people in their activities. Kidsactive is another organisation which sees the need for providing recreation facilities in the community and as well as specialising in running adventure playgrounds for disabled children they also offer training, advice and consultancy for groups and organisations. They campaign for equal rights to play opportunities for *all* children, run six adventure playgrounds in the London area, and through training and publications encourage others to take up the challenge. To learn more about the work of these organisations and for contact details see Resources, Part 2.

Finally, it is worth taking the initiative and contacting local schools of art, architecture, planning or music and drama to enquire about the opportunities for students and schools to develop projects together. Large orchestras or other branches of the arts may also have funding for projects with people with learning disabilities and unless teachers approach them they may not know where the needs are or who would be interested in what they have to offer. A creative, imaginative approach and a high level of commitment will be needed if teachers are to recognise the learning possibilities outside school, and it is worth remembering that wherever the curriculum is delivered, to quote Brown *et al.* (1998 p. 34) 'overwhelmingly, for most learners with PMLD and sensory impairments, the most important part of the environment will be the people in contact with them at a particular time'.

Suggested further reading

Reading material for parents

Mencap (and Partners) (1999) – see Bibliography.

RNIB (1995) *Play it my way: learning through play with your visually impaired child.* UK: HMSO.

The *Fulton Special Educational Digest: selected resources for teachers, parents and carers,* edited by Ann Worthington, is a useful resource to have in school and is available directly from David Fulton Publishers (020 7405 5606) or from Winslow. The Winslow catalogue has reading material for parents about specific conditions.

An approach to recognising and responding to pupil's natural and unprompted responses has been produced on video by Bronwen Burford (1990), and there is a booklet on the same subject produced by the Health Promotion Research Trust (U/D) entitled *Children with Profound Handicaps: How carers can communicate through movement.*

Many publications from the Royal Institute for the Blind are aimed at both teachers and parents. Although the primary audience is for those working with children with visual impairment, there is a section in their catalogue for pupils with PMLD, with a strong emphasis on a sensory approach to learning.

CHAPTER 6

Integration for all pupils

At the time of writing, £20 million has been allocated through the Schools Access Initiative to make 1,600 mainstream schools more accessible to disabled pupils and those with sensory impairments. This will be the start of a £100 million programme over the next three years. Co-located sites for special and mainstream schools are becoming increasingly common and the curriculum has been revised to provide effective learning opportunities for all pupils, with a statutory statement on inclusion. However, it is important to bear in mind the original perceived need for special schools which was the beginning of inclusion, not exclusion. It would be all too easy for some pupils to be viewed as unable to benefit from any learning with their mainstream peers and for them yet again to become an isolated group. Two case studies are offered as examples of schools that are working at including their PMLD pupils with their mainstream peers. The first case study centres on a special school that has been on a co-located site for many years and is starting to explore the educational possibilities of the integration of pupils with complex needs with their mainstream peers. The second case study focuses on a school that has devoted a great deal of time and commitment to establishing and nurturing educational links with a wide range of schools within its area. Many of the issues surrounding the subject of inclusion will be covered in these studies, and for this reason it was decided to describe the work of these schools in particular detail.

Case Study 1

Context

Bishopswood School is a Special School for pupils with severe and profound and multiple learning difficulties. It is co-located with mainstream schools on three sites and this case study centres on the primary department at Sonning Common in

Oxfordshire. Some pupils integrate into Sonning Common Primary School on a regular basis and all Bishopswood children attend their assembly on Friday mornings. They share a playground and there are opportunities for social integration, but for the pupils with PMLD any real inclusion has been very limited. The team leader for Bishopswood School had for some time been enthusiastic about forging closer links with the mainstream primary school. When the school received funding from Oxfordshire County Council to develop 'Action Research Projects' relating to 'Inclusion within the SEN Standards Fund' this gave the team leader the chance she needed. It was decided to use the money to fund extra Learning Support Assistant (LSA) time to help with integration.

Aims of the project

The stated aims are:

- for *every* Bishopswood pupil to have access to mainstream provision;
- to extend inclusion opportunities through improved staff links;
- to take advantage of suitable activities/learning experiences.

Action

It was decided that for the first term it would be good to explore ways in which the literacy hour could be a shared experience for a mainstream class and a small group of pupils with PMLD. The first task was to convince the Year 4 teacher from Sonning Common Primary School that this could be fitted into an already crowded curriculum. This teacher was also concerned about how her pupils would react and whether they would be too embarrassed to perform. Once it was agreed that it was worth 'having a go', a time was fixed for the Bishopswood teacher to talk to the mainstream pupils about the children in her class and the nature of their special needs. It was explained that in order for pupils with PMLD to understand and enjoy a story there would have to be extra sensory input. The Year 4 pupils were full of ideas as to how this could be done and very enthusiastic about the whole project.

The following week the Bishopswood teacher found four stories with repetitive phrases which lent themselves to sensory input. She prepared boxes for each story with suggested props and the mainstream teacher divided the class into four groups. Each group was given a book and an accompanying box of props and, with some adult guidance, they read through the story, decided on a narrator and chose the props they would need. It was decided that a different group would tell their story each week. There was a limited time for practice with the LSA before the 'performance' and a brief discussion time afterwards. Each group had a second turn which gave them a chance to review what worked and what did not work the first time round.

Feedback

1. *Bishopswood staff:* There was very enthusiastic feedback from staff and parents. Some stories had worked better than others. To some extent this depended on the dynamics of the group of storytellers, but familiar stories with a simple theme and plenty of repetition were the most successful and easiest for beginners to put across. An added bonus for Bishopswood staff was a build up of resources for use in the literacy hour. The most difficult part was fitting in with the mainstream timetable.

2. *LSA support:* The LSA had not worked with pupils with PMLD before and had enjoyed seeing their responses. She was very impressed by how well the mainstream pupils had grasped the needs of the pupils with PMLD. Some fruitful discussions resulted from these mixed group sessions and these would have been even more successful if there had been more time for planning and feedback.

3. *Mainstream teacher:* Doubts had been dispelled – the children had performed well, even the shy ones. Sharing the sensory experiences had necessitated the children getting close to one another, whereas in the playground they tended to keep their distance. Barriers had broken down. She was now able to see the possibilities of building integrated activities into the mainstream curriculum and identified areas that had been covered during the project to include English (in particular, speaking and listening), drama, music, problem solving, art and design, design and technology, self-evaluation, religious education and human values education.

Way forward

It was decided to free-up LSA support from Bishopswood to keep the integration links going for pupils with PMLD and to target Year 4 classes each year. It was also resolved to:

- start with the learning needs of the pupils;
- plan and build activities into the module for the term;
- plan activities as a timetabled part of the curriculum – it does not work if integration is seen as an extra activity to be fitted in;
- aim for 'inclusion', with PMLD pupils contributing to the sessions as part of a two-way process;
- extend activities for mainstream pupils to include writing their own material, making their own props, composing a sound track or making a video of the performance.

Case Study 2

Frank Wise School, in Banbury, is an Oxfordshire County Council School for pupils aged 2 to 16 with severe learning difficulties. A significant proportion of the pupils have profound and multiple learning difficulties and are fully integrated within the school, which groups strictly according to chronological age. Michael Thompson was the deputy head teacher at the time of writing and, although he has since moved on, another teacher has taken on responsibility for links with the school on which this study is based. Michael has a particular interest in integration and he has taken an 'encouragement' role, but every class teacher has responsibility for liaising with their partner school and for keeping integration links with mainstream well-established. At present, all classes at Frank Wise School have an educational integration link with a school in the local community for at least one morning or afternoon a week. A total of seven mainstream schools are involved and no pupil is excluded. Activities are carefully planned and national curriculum based. This study centres round Year 5/6 class from Frank Wise School and their parallel class in Greatworth Primary School – a small village school of 120 pupils just across the county border in Northamptonshire with which there have been links for the past ten years.

Michael has strong views about integration versus inclusion although he is keen to stress that these opinions are personal. He says that, ideally, in a perfect world, all pupils, no matter how profound their degree of difficulty, should be able to be educated in a non-segregated mainstream environment where all their special educational needs are appropriately and effectively met. He acknowledges that the resource, training and expertise implications of this are enormous, but really believes that special schools exist primarily for economical reasons. However, if, economically and politically, full inclusion is out of the question, Michael says that pupils with complex needs still have the right to learn alongside their mainstream peers for at least some of their school week. He would not define being educated in a special unit on the mainstream school site as real 'inclusion'. He says that, invariably, when you look closely at such arrangements, there is a pocket of more challenging pupils, usually those with PMLD, who have been 'ghettoised' to segregated provision elsewhere, or if they *are* included, never leave the unit. To him, inclusion means provision where *all* pupils, regardless of their severity of need, are educated in their chronological age group in a mainstream school, with their special educational needs being effectively met. Frank Wise and Greatworth schools start planning projects from the premise that *everyone* is going to be involved and this works in practice by 'differentiating up'. When planning for residential trips, each venue is checked first for curricular opportunities for the pupils with PMLD, and the rest of the programme works around this.

When staff first become involved in integration projects there can be some anxiety on both sides. The larger class sizes are a little daunting for the Frank Wise staff and the challenging behaviour of some of the Frank Wise pupils can cause the Greatworth staff to feel apprehensive. Communication between schools is all important and there is a written strategy for dealing with severely challenging behaviour to which staff in both schools adhere. The reasoning behind this strategy is explained to the mainstream class, giving the thinking behind it, when the pupils in question are not there. Michael says that it would be a mistake, however, to assume that the challenging behaviour always comes from the special school children – Greatworth teachers have sought advice on behavioural management from them for their own pupils, with successful results. He notes that it is interesting how quickly the frame of reference in conversations between the two groups of staff shifts from differences to similarities once they have got to know each other. It is worth re-emphasising that *no* pupil is excluded from integration schemes.

There are other ways in which the benefits of links between the schools have been two-way. In analysing how the PMLD pupils learn, it has made mainstream pupils more aware of how they themselves learn. At several of the integration link schools they have taken 'communication' as the termly focus for the whole class and the subtleties of early communication from the PMLD pupils has been analysed and interpreted. Use of symbol and signing systems has also been an important theme and mainstream pupils have enjoyed inventing their own. The sensory curriculum has been beneficial to mainstream pupils in two-way integration links, where groups from partner schools have been able to come to Frank Wise to explore their light and sound stimulation studio and their hydrotherapy pool. These are just some examples, but generally they have found that once the mainstream pupils have realised that sensory experiences are a key to learning for the PMLD pupils, they themselves look for opportunities to provide these. This has been particularly noticeable on residential trips where mainstream pupils have gone out of their way to discover the sensory potential of each location.

Joint projects are planned, and for these there is a long and successful history of buying in artists in residence and other outside expertise for integration work. Examples include a choreographer, an Asian dance teacher, a ceramicist, a woodcarver, a poet and 'Fairport Convention'! There is some flexibility with Frank Wise staff and they have occasionally swapped round if they needed a good musician or an artist or a PE specialist for an ongoing project. Parents from both schools are also very keen on the integration links, and by and large they recognise the enormous benefits. They help with special projects out of school times, acting as make-up artists, taxi drivers and scenery builders. Extra assistance is also given by teacher training students who are given a small honorarium to help on residential trips. When asked if things ever go wrong, Michael said that lots of things haven't worked but if the link is strong the determination is there to put them right. He has discovered that integration goes less well when the mainstream school is seen as the 'host' and the Frank Wise class as the visitors, and it works best when there is shared responsibility for planning and teaching. He says that occasionally they have made the mistake of trying to do too much and of making the projects too complicated – it is possible to be ambitious and simple.

To summarise

Writing in *PMLD Link* (Autumn 1999) Michael Thompson identifies key principles for setting up an integration link, summarised thus:

1. Most importantly, establish right from the outset that the integration link is to be educational with a clear curriculum focus at all times.
2. Go slowly at first, find an opportunity for teachers to visit each other's classes.
3. Initial contact between the two school classes should be fun – choose a curriculum area which is a favourite of both classes.
4. Share planning and teaching equally between the two teachers plus any support staff.
5. Wherever possible, each term or half term's work should have a tangible outcome such as a video, joint display or performance.
6. Plan early for the next academic year to build the integration link into the timetabling and long-term planning for both schools.
7. Be committed to making sure that integration *will* take place and will not be cancelled to make room for something 'more important'. Establish this principle from the outset.

Suggested further reading

Alderson, P. (1999) (ed.) *Learning and Inclusion: The Cleves School Experience.* London: David Fulton Publishers.

Tamaren, M. (1991) *I Make a Difference! A Curriculum Guide to Building Self-Esteem and Sensitivity in the Classroom.* Ann Arbor: Ann Arbor Publications.

CHAPTER 7

Literacy and numeracy in regular timetabled subjects

With the introduction of *The National Literacy Strategy* (DfEE 1998) and *The National Numeracy Strategy* (DfEE 1999) there has been greater emphasis in England on the teaching of these subjects. Frameworks for teaching suggest that primary school children will have an hour of literacy a day and a daily mathematics lesson lasting between 45 minutes and an hour. Although this is not a legal requirement, it is expected that *all* children will benefit from these structured teaching sessions.

Both the literacy strategy and the numeracy strategy acknowledge that a small minority of pupils may need to start at a level below their Key Stage and that for literacy this may be below Reception Level. It would seem realistic to use the key objectives at Reception Level in both subjects as the starting point for planning for pupils with PMLD. These have therefore been included alongside the appropriate NC objectives on the Curriculum document pages in Part 2 of this book. Although nothing specific is said about pupils for whom the Reception Level or below may be appropriate throughout their school life, it is acknowledged in the *National Numeracy Strategy* (p. 24) that 'extra "small steps" may need to be inserted and contexts for practical work and problem-solving adapted for the pupils' ages'. Perhaps the greatest benefit for pupils with PMLD is the opportunity offered to teachers to reassess what should be taught and to allow for systematic planning over a school year.

However, there are difficulties that will need to be addressed before taking both strategies on board without careful consideration. Pupils with physical and learning difficulties need a calm and unrushed day and allowance needs to be made for the time taken for moving from one place to another, changes of position, everyday care and the inevitable interruptions. If teachers attempt to add daily specific literacy and numeracy lessons to an already busy timetable, other important areas of the curriculum will be pushed out. However, if the core of literacy is communication as stressed by Olga Miller (1999), and if we view mathematical language and concepts as needing to be experienced bodily through the senses, the way is opened up to using existing timetabled activities to provide opportunities for both group and individual teaching of the core subjects. It will be important to be able to prove that pupils are receiving literacy and numeracy teaching on a daily basis, but it does not always have to be in a single block and a range of activities can be used to deliver these subjects.

The National Numeracy Strategy and supplement of examples at Reception Level offers activities to help children reach identified key objectives, some of which can be adapted to suit pupils with PMLD and the Curriculum document in Part 2 of this book has further ideas for a sensory approach to the teaching of mathematics. The accompanying DfEE book on mathematical vocabulary informs of language that children need to grasp in order to understand mathematical concepts. For pupils with complex needs these concepts will need to be experienced through body shapes and movement, and all physical programmes such as exercise sessions, structured games in the swimming pool, activities in the soft play area, music and movement, Sherborne movement and group times on the resonance board can be used for the teaching of mathematics. If key language is used consistently by all adults concerned, pupils will experience and develop the 'feel' of concepts such as:

far	under	between
near	circle	opposite
up	in front	apart
down	behind	towards
high	front	away from
low	back	bigger
in	beside	smaller
out	next to	turn and stretch

Timetabled activities can also be used to plan lessons concentrating on specific learning targets for literacy and numeracy. News-telling sessions give natural opportunities for delivering literacy, as is demonstrated in Figure 7.1.

For other lessons the emphasis could change from week to week. This is demonstrated in Figures 7.2 and 7.3 where a baking session could be used to deliver either the literacy hour or the numeracy hour, and the same exercise could be done for the delivery of science. Recording will reflect the teaching priorities of each lesson and adults working with the children will be given clear guidance as to what to be looking for in individual pupils. This book is concentrating on the needs of pupils with the most profound learning difficulties, but for pupils who are ready for the next stage, Berger *et al.* (2000) give a breakdown of the 11 key objectives for Reception for the National Numeracy Framework and offer ideas for planning teaching in a mixed ability class.

Location/situation	Activity	Resources*
Classroom A group of eight pupils with either SLD or PMLD Grouped round the table Working individually Re-grouped round table	Greet each pupil in turn. Pupils tell their news in turn using one or more of the following methods – verbally, by signing, using a personal communication board or using a switch device on which their news has been recorded. Ensure pupils are listening to each other and encourage discussion. Pupils to record their news in a variety of ways, for example: • With help, cut out symbols (printed out or drawn by adult during news session) and stick in their news book. • Use Writing with Symbols (pupils who are able to use this can record another pupil's news for them). • Copy writing and draw picture. Adult to show work to the group and read each pupil's news in turn.	Home school diaries Recordable switch devices such as AbleNet, BIGmack (Inclusive Technology) or Talking Buddy (Cambridge Adaptive Communication) More advanced hand-held aids to communication such as Mini-Message Mate (Words + Inc.) Personal communication boards Individual news books Software such as Writing with Symbols 2000 (Inclusive Technology) Writing and drawing materials

* Reference details and contact information can be found in Resources section (Part 2)

Figure 7.1 Delivering the literacy hour in a group news-telling session

Curriculum area and learning targets	Activities and resources
Pupils should be able to: *English: Speaking and Listening:* Develop skills of swallowing, chewing, licking, lip closure	Eating the cake.
Communicate needs	Show pleasure/displeasure. 'Ask' for cake/refuse cake.
Locate sounds Track sounds	All the different 'cooking' sounds – note whether pupil looks towards sound.
Use interactive equipment	Press switch to use electric food mixer/whisk.
English: Reading Use visual clues to give meaning to activities and events Make a link between object and photograph Make a link between object and symbol Recognise photographs of self and familiar people Enjoy and respond to looking at books	Use chosen object of reference to indicate that 'baking' is on the timetable. Make books that go through each step for making a cake. Use pictures and photographs of equipment and ingredients – supermarket magazines have good, clear photographs. Make individual books with photographs of the pupil and others in the group doing the cooking. Include real ingredients where suitable, e.g. spices to smell, sugar and raisins to feel.
English: Writing Participate in making marks on surfaces	Pupils can help to dribble icing over cake in a pattern or decorate with sugar strands.

Figure 7.2 Using activities in a baking session to deliver the literacy hour

Curriculum area and learning targets	Activities and resources
Pupils should be able to:	
Mathematics: Using and Applying Relate objects to their functions	Cooking utensils, oven – what are they for? What do we do with them?
Mathematics: Shape, Space and Measures Show an awareness of similarities in properties of objects and materials Show an awareness of opposite properties of objects and materials	Tins, saucepan etc. – all metal. Metal spoons/wooden spoons. Rough sugar/smooth flour.
When handling objects, show an awareness of differences in shape, size or weight	Feel the shape of the tins. Feel weights, bags of sugar, flour etc. Feel difference in weight between empty and full containers.
Use sensory clues to build up a picture of the environment	Cooking sounds. Cooking smells. Warmth of oven. Warmth and smell of baked cake.
Mathematics: Number Develop an awareness of rote counting	Count the number in the group. How many pieces of cake do we need? Cut cake and count pieces. Have we got enough? Count as cake is handed round.

Figure 7.3 Using activities in a baking session to deliver numeracy

Suggested further reading

The reading materials listed under this heading in Chapters 2 and 8 are relevant here.

CHAPTER 8

Access to literature for pupils with PMLD

Our approach to teaching literature to students who may be able neither to read or write, nor to understand much of what is read to them, will be determined by the way we conceptualise the subject: as an aspect of literacy, an aspect of language or a form of art.

(Grove 1998 p. 9)

The *National Literacy Strategy* (DfEE 1998) emphasises the place of literature as a means of helping students to develop reading and writing skills. Taking this narrow view of the subject will exclude pupils with PMLD who struggle enough with making sense of everyday events in the world around them. However, as already discussed in Chapter 7, for pupils with profound learning difficulties, the core of literacy is communication. When adults acknowledge this and are prepared to adapt the way in which literature is presented, pupils can be helped to understand that books have meaning and that stories and poetry give enjoyment. The quote at the beginning of this chapter prompts us to examine our reasons for the teaching of literature and we will look at each aspect of the subject.

Literature as an aspect of literacy

Objects of reference, pictorial and symbolic representation

Objects of reference may be the first introduction to 'reading' words for pupils with PMLD. These were first used with pupils who were deaf or blind but have since been found to be useful for pupils with PMLD, regardless of whether or not they have a hearing or visual impairment. An 'object of reference' is something which has a particular meaning associated with it for an individual child. Park (1999/2000) states that 'objects need to be relevant to the individual user and not to the therapist, teacher or inspector'. He says that objects which are chosen must be meaningful and motivating for the individual child and something that is frequently used. For this reason, food or favourite activities are often a good starting point – for example a personal spoon, bowl or cup can be used to indicate time for dinner or a drink, or a favourite team scarf may 'say' that it is time to watch football live or on television. By using the same object consistently, it can come to represent the activity, person or event. If more than one sense is involved the message will be reinforced and it may be convenient to keep objects in wallets with accompanying smells, textures or visual effects. For example, the smell of herbs or gravy granules can help to indicate 'dinner', a torch shining on diffraction paper can indicate darkroom activities and the feel of sandpaper and the smell of woodshavings can indicate 'woodwork'.

It is generally agreed that, at the first level, the whole identical object is shown to the pupil and when there is sufficient understanding a part of the object or an object which is the same but different can be introduced. Later on the object could be represented in a tactile way on a piece of card and this will lead eventually to symbolic representation in the form of photographs, pictures and symbols – symbol systems most frequently used with pupils with PMLD are Makaton, Rebus and Picture Communication Symbols (PCS). However, if symbols are used alongside real objects, parts of objects, photographs or pictures from the beginning and throughout the day, understanding may filter through gradually.

At the first stage objects of reference will be used to help pupils to make sense of their environment but at the final stage they will used for intentional communication. Objects of reference, personal to the child, can be used by an adult to inform of a change of activity or used by the child to make a particular request. For group activities objects can be shared and used across school and home environments. Objects can be displayed on a reference board and used to talk the whole class through the timetable for the day, for example a towel can indicate swimming, a textured rubber mat can indicate that it is time to exercise and bells can indicate that music is the next lesson. There are suggestions for further reading on the use of objects of reference at the end of this chapter.

Objects of reference, pictorial and symbolic representation in non-fiction

The *National Literacy Strategy* (DfEE 1998) describes non-fiction as 'non-fiction texts, including recounts' and says that, in particular, the skills focusing on reading and writing non-fiction texts should be linked to and applied to every subject. The most successful books will be 'home made', building on the interests of the individual child or the group, with objects of reference, textures, smells, photos, pictures and symbols. Figures 7.1 and 7.2 in Chapter 7 suggested ways of using books in regular, timetabled activities, and further possibilities could include:

- personal books about family and home life, journey to school, favourite things etc.;

- books which can be used to give choices;
- recipe books for cookery lessons (using photos, pictures, symbols, real ingredients such as raisins, spices etc. sprinkled onto glue);
- shopping lists with objects of reference, pictures, photos, food labels, symbols, smells etc.;
- books about regular walks, e.g. to the shops, (these could include photos, objects of reference, textures, smells, road signs etc.);
- books to record outings, with as much sensory input as possible. An audiotape, with memorable sounds, can accompany the book to help pupils recall the visit;
- class book to record activities based on the topic for the term;
- individual records for the term with photos, samples of work to include computer printouts, art work etc.

Objects of reference, pictorial and symbolic representation in fiction
Chris Fuller (Bag Books) has explored the use of objects and associated sensory clues in storytelling and poetry and has produced books in an unconventional form for communicating with pupils with PMLD (see Figure 8.2, the Resources section in Part 2 and Suggested further reading at the end of this chapter). Examples of his work can be found in *Reading for All* (Mencap 1999) and his materials will stimulate teachers to come up with their own ideas for making storytelling come alive. Keith Park has used objects of reference in storytelling and one example is his interactive version of *Oliver Twist* (see under Access to books . . . in the Resources section of Part 2). It will be relatively easy to find books which lend themselves to storytelling with young children, but a lot of adaptation will be needed if older students are to have the opportunity to access adult literature – this will be discussed further later in this chapter and in Chapter 9. As with non-fiction literature, some of the best storybooks are those made by an adult who is familiar with the child or young person and Figures 8.1 and 8.2 suggest aids to storytelling to include ready made materials. For the more ambitious it is worth obtaining catalogues from suppliers such as SEMERC and PCS for aids for personalising pictures and symbols.

Mencap (1999) have a section on 'Making your own stories' and it is inspiring to see the possibilities for sensory input when adults use their imagination.

Pupil input into storytelling

Pupils should be given the opportunity to join in with stories and to influence the storyline. There is plenty of sophisticated technology to aid pupils to communicate in this way, but cheaper options may be just as effective (see Figure 8.3). Some pupils may be able to access further elements of literacy with appropriate software, and Figure 8.4 lists available materials. In a mixed ability class this may be a good chance for pupils to work in pairs.

For those wanting a more detailed approach to teaching literacy to pupils with learning difficulties, Berger *et al.* (1999) offer comprehensive advice on how the learning objectives of the NLS can be broken down into small steps, with suggestions for activities to enable pupils to achieve these steps.

Literature as an aspect of language

Grove (1998 p. 15) says that children 'enjoy language as a form of play from a very early age, manipulating sounds, rhythm and tones of voice'. She also concludes from research that young children use various cues to pick up the meaning of words, and these include stress and intonation, familiarity with a structured framework, associations with familiar routines and events and an emotional response to the text. Pupils of all ages, functioning at an early developmental level, will respond to language in a similar way. When literature is adapted to provide enjoyment of words, regardless of the level of comprehension, and when emotions are shared between the storyteller and the listener, even adult literature can be experienced and enjoyed by pupils with complex needs. Nicola Grove and Keith Park are two authors who have worked on taking classical poetry and literature and making it available to pupils who need a sensory approach to learning, and this will be explored further in Chapter 9. A list of such adapted literature can be found under 'Access to books for pupils with sensory impairment' in Resources (Part 2).

It is worth exploring how other professionals have approached the language aspect of literacy with pupils with PMLD. Music is an effective access route to pupils with the most profound learning difficulties and the pattern of poetry can be experienced through singing rhymes or rap rhythm. Professionals working with the resonance board are usually trained musicians and work in an exciting way on the aspects of language already identified as important for pupils with profound learning difficulties. They play with words, sounds and rhythms in group settings, tapping on bodies, the resonance board, table, floor, drums or other percussion instruments. The leader is guided by the response of the children, which is often strong, and in the silences provided pupils join in by making their own individual sounds. Activities can include storytelling and poetry and this is often improvised according to the situation and the interests of individual children. It is impossible to describe the full extent of the work of such organisations but contact information can be found in Resources (Part 2). It will be valuable for staff to see a session in action and if possible to receive training in all the possibilities opened up by this way of working.

Literature as an aspect of art

Mencap (1999 p. 23) suggest that the choice of books should be governed by the needs and likes of children with PMLD and identify particular preferences as including: 'sudden surprises; opportunities for contrasting sounds and smells; gentle, rhythmical words; possibilities for joining in and spaces for dramatic pauses'. This immediately opens up the idea of storytelling and poetry being more than an aspect of literacy, as has already been identified in the previous sections. An understanding of books as a means of communication, and the use of technology to assist in joining in with storytelling and to gain access to further elements of literacy, is important, but for some pupils these concepts may always be too difficult, even when aids to communication are employed. Real enjoyment of literature may only be possible when the story is 'felt' through the emotions and this will require adults involved with the students to view literature as, above all, an aspect of art.

There is evidence to suggest that regardless of the degree of cognitive impairment or delay, emotional memories can still be evoked, and Grove (1998) quotes Goleman (1996 p. 10) as saying that 'The fact that the thinking brain grew from the emotional reveals much about the relationship of thought to feeling: there was an emotional brain long before there was a thinking one'. This would suggest that when sensations and feelings are involved, nobody needs to be excluded from an enjoyment of stories, poetry and drama – this will be followed up in Chapter 9 when exploring the place of drama in the curriculum. Any aspect of the arts requires audience participation and relies on building a relationship between the 'players' and the public, and these are requirements for storytelling with pupils with PMLD. To quote Mencap (1999 p. 103), 'the whole point of storytelling the world over is that there should be delight in the telling and sharing. Nothing else really matters'.

Suggested resources*	Description/ideas for using
Booklist in *Reading for All* (Mencap 1999). See Resources in Part 2 of this book.	Recommended story books. Books that lend themselves to dramatic presentation.
The Children's Bookselling Group at the Booksellers Association.	For a list of specialist children's bookshops.
Wordless Picture Books (REACH).	Suitable for pupils of all ages including teenagers.
REACH National Advice Centre.	Over 8,000 children's books in print, sound and vision (and lots more).
Simple Symbol Stories by Pati King-DeBaun (Mayer-Johnson Co.) *Storytime* *Storytime, Just for Fun* *Storytime, Holiday Fun!*	Interactive stories combined with suggested related activities. Interactive story units with finger plays, folk tales and creative projects. Language boards are provided. Includes props, songs and supplemental displays.
Hands on Reading, *More Hands on Reading* by Jane Kelly and Theresa Friend (Mayer-Johnson Co.).	Symbols, music, props, art, cooking ideas etc. to accompany popular children's books that can be found in libraries and bookshops.
Story Cards from Winslow.	Pack of four animal stories with four finger puppets. Stories are on accompanying cards.
Adaptations of classic books – see Keith Park's list under Interactive story telling (Resources). Teacher manual for accessing *Romeo and Juliet* by Grove and Park (contact Bag Books).	Example – *Odyssey Now, A Christmas Carol, Little Red Riding Hood, Cinderella, Romeo and Juliet, Hansel and Gretel, Joseph, Oliver Twist, Macbeth in Mind.*
Stories from Bag Books – *The Hot Air Balloon* (poem), *The Party, Desmond's Gran's Visit, Maria's Ball, The Bookseller* – also a video to show the stories being told.	Story packs with accompanying objects for making the stories come 'alive'.
Multisensory fiction for teenagers – *The Match, The First Day, It's cold INSIDE!, Jason's Wish* (Bag Books). See also Keith Park's list as above.	Multisensory stories with teenage interest with accompanying contents as above.
Books beyond Words series. Sovereign series – from Book Sales Department, Royal College of Psychiatrists.	Books for older pupils which include issues such as 'A New Home in the Community', 'When Dad Died' and 'Hugging and Kissing'.
Symbol Stories (Widget Software).	Symbol stories created for older pupils with learning difficulties and available to subscribers.
Story/Symbol Pack (CALL Centre).	Good storybooks for younger children that can be bought individually or in a pack – each book comes with pictures for sticking on the top of a BIGmack.

*Reference details and contact information can be found in Resources (Part 2)

Figure 8.1 Group story telling: Ideas for reading books

Suggested resources*	Description/ideas for using
Signing system such as Makaton.	Sign the most important words – especially those already familiar to the pupils. Keep it simple!
Big book stand (LDA).	Easy to store double-sided stand. One side holds the book and the other side is a magnetic white board for magnetic objects or markers.
Teaching backcloth (LDA). Large magnetic board on stand (TFH). Velcro board (TFH). A magnetic story board (Winslow).	Felt – for displaying pictures, symbols, objects. For own use – magnetic tape from TFH. Velcro board in frame to hang or lie flat. Pictorial scene with 40 magnetic pieces.
Beat That! and Soundabout materials, also training for staff. Start with your best resource – imagination, enthusiasm and good knowledge of your own pupils. Practise making up stories and rhymes about events throughout the day. Build stories around individual children.	These organisations have ideas for using rhythmic sounds to encourage listening and communication skills. Sounds can be enhanced by using a resonance board, table, floor, drums or bodies. Rap rhythm can be used to tell impromptu stories or poems with a beat. Make it fun!
Multisensory stories from Bag Books. Tango Books.	Not in conventional book form. Each page is an A3 laminated card to which an object is attached – objects can be felt, listened to or smelt as the story goes along.
A Do-it-yourself Guide to Making Six Tactile Books by Chris Fuller. This manual can be obtained from Bag Books.	Instructions for props needed for telling simple stories and large laminated story cards. Not too childish and can be adapted for making your own stories (see also Reading for All Mencap 1999 pp. 53–63).
Contact National Play Information Centre.	Will give information about local scrapbank with materials for making your own tactile books.
See Reading for All Mencap (1999) pp. 16–18 and 64–8 for further ideas for making and using home made books.	Contains further ideas for making and using home made books.
Story boxes – make your own.	Objects collected to accompany a print book, such as toy bears, chairs , bowls and beds for Goldilocks and the Three Bears.
Memory boxes – make your own.	A story box made up of souvenirs (tactile, noisy, smelly) to accompany a class book about an outing.
Hands on Reading More Hands on Reading by Jane Kelly and Theresa Friend (Mayer-Johnson Co.).	Symbols, music, props, art, cooking ideas etc. to accompany popular children's books that can be found in libraries and bookshops.
Puppets – e.g. 'Molly' (LDA catalogue) – see the Resource section in Part 2 for more ideas.	A large puppet with features which enable signing, different mouth shapes and tongue positioning.

*Reference details and contact information can be found in Resources (Part 2)

Figure 8.2 Group story telling: Aids to storytelling.

Technology*	Description/ideas for using
Etran frame (QED 2000) or Eye-Comboard (Winslow) Perspex frame with no centre. Objects, photos, pictures or symbols are attached to the perimeter.	Adult sits opposite the child and can see where eyes are pointing (Etran frame) or where pointer is indicating.
The Comboard (Tash International Inc. – available from Cambridge Adaptive Communication), is a picture symbol communication board with a pointer activated by a single switch. Pointer is rotated until it reaches the desired picture/symbol.	Talk through the story and ask child to indicate what comes next or which bit they would like again. If choice is random respond as if it was intentional and repeat that part of the story until the pupil understands that *they* can choose.
Message communication devices for pre-recording repetitive parts of story or relevant sounds.	Recordings can be played back by the child at the right place in the story.
BIGmack (Inclusive Technology and others).	A one message communication device – press top to play.
Talking Buddy (Cambridge Adaptive Communication).	As above (15 seconds of recording time).
Untouchable Buddy (Cambridge Adaptive Communication).	A 'no-hands' switch which can be customised to allow access by approximate motions or touch.
Most battery-operated toys may be adapted by the use of a battery device adaptor placed between the battery and the terminal in the battery of the toy. These adaptors are inexpensive and available from most software catalogues. See TFH for adapted toys. For companies specialising in the supply of toys for children with disabilities and for High Street stores with toys which can be easily adapted for switch use see the Liberator: Simple Technology Catalogue.	Switches can be used to control: • mains or battery devices • domestic appliances • speech output systems • toys • computers. A good range of switches – Tash catalogue. Switch latch and timers – Liberator. Unusual switches – TFH catalogue. Pupils can operate toys or other appliances to illustrate the story.
Soundbeam attached to musical keyboard. An invisible beam which, when broken, enables a person to play the keyboard. Very small motions are needed to break the beam.	Position the beam to suit individual movements and choose a style of music to suit the mood of the story. Contact Soundabout for training in use of the soundbeam.
Equipment to amplify the pupil's sounds such as: karaoke machine, microphone, Zube tube.	Encourage pupils to 'shout' into an instrument and join in with exciting parts of the story.
Resonance board – a flat wooden board raised slightly off the ground. Pupils are placed on the board or around the edge and any movements, tapping or banging will be amplified. Can be purchased through Soundabout.	Pupils are often vocal in the stillness after a drumming session on the board and this may be a good time to amplify or record their sounds. Try telling stories such as *The Billy Goats Gruff* or *Let's go on a Lion Hunt*, using the board to make sound effects.

*There are explanations in the Glossary and reference details and contact information in Resources (Part 2). Note that most of the technology can be found in several catalogues, not only those quoted.

Figure 8.3 Extended activities: Technology to assist pupils with PMLD to join in with storytelling

Software*	Description/suggestions for use
Blob for Windows (Widgit Software): • Blob 1 • Blob 2	A pack with 10 separate activities in two sets. Designed to introduce switch control and the concept of cause and effect. Attractive graphics and each game is on a number of levels to help progression.
Make it Happen 1, 2, and 3 (Widgit Software).	For students with severe difficulties coming to the computer for the first time.
Early Years • The Switch On series • First Steps • The Touch games series • Sound Stuff *Sensory Software* • Build IT (and support packs) All available from SEMERC – obtain catalogue for full software range	Just bash a switch to make something happen! For Touch screen 24 animated pictures of everyday objects and the sounds they make. Each switch press creates sound and reveals more of the picture. The graphics on these programmes would make them suitable for pupils of all ages.
Smart Alex (Brilliant Computing, available from SEMERC).	A big cartoon character that talks, cries, laughs, blows raspberries, plus many other actions – particularly suitable for older pupils.
Animations. *Radsounds* (from Liberator: Simple Technology).	101 colourful animations – works with a mouse click or single switch. Radical animations and sounds – for early switch users. The cartoons are non-age specific making these programmes suitable for all ages.
Rainbow Stories (Inclusive Technology).	18 talking and singing books of favourite stories – mouse, touchscreen or keyboard.
Sensory Software (Inclusive Technology).	A set of programmes developed for pupils with PMLD.
Touch (Inclusive Technology).	Touch the colourful shapes to see/hear the reward.
Switchit! series (Inclusive Technology) – At home; Diggers; Gadgets; Patterns.	Switch operated cause and effect software appropriate for learners of all ages.

*Details of suppliers can be found in Resources (Part 2).

For a wide range of switches see the Tash International catalogue, available from Cambridge Adaptive Communication. For unusual switches see TFH.

Note that most of the software can be obtained from a range of catalogues, including those quoted.

Figure 8.4 Software to aid pupils with PMLD to gain access to further elements of literacy

Suggested further reading

Fuller, C. (1999) 'Bag Books Tactile Stories', *The SLD Experience*, **23**, 20–1.
Grove, N. (1998) – see Bibliography.
Berger A. *et al.* (1999) – see Bibliography.

The following articles in *PMLD Link* **12** (1), (Winter 1999/2000) are recommended reading:
Park, K. 'Reading objects: Literacy and Objects of Reference'.
Fuller, C. 'Fiction for Adults with Profound and Multiple Learning Difficulties'.
Patel, B. 'Making the Most of your Library'.
Aird, R. and Heath, S. 'The Teaching of English and Literacy to Secondary Aged Pupils with Profound and Multiple Learning Difficulties'.
Lambe, H. and Walters, S. 'Homework Packs/Toy Library'.
Atkins, S. 'Students with Profound and Multiple Learning Difficulties Enjoy the Literacy Hour'.

Likewise the following articles in *Eye Contact* (RNIB) **23** (Spring 1999) will prove useful:
Miller, O. 'The National Literacy Strategy and pupils with visual impairment and multiple disabilities'.
Nolan, B. 'Literacy Hour – a positive approach'.
Everard, M. 'A story with a tactile trail'.

Information technology and symbols

For information about every ICT device you can think of consult:
Rumble, G. and Larcher, J. (1998) 'AAC Device Review' (available from Vocation, West House, Berwick Road, Marlow SL7 3AR. Tel: 01628 488911).
Detheridge, T. and Detheridge, M. (1997) *Literacy through Symbols: Improving access for children and adults*. London: David Fulton Publishers.

Objects of reference

Ockleford, A. (1993) *Objects of Reference: Promoting concept development and communication skills with visually impaired children who have learning difficulties.* London: RNIB.
Park, K. (1997) 'How do Objects become Objects of Reference? – A review of literature on objects of reference and a proposed model for the use of objects in communication', *British Journal of Special Education* **24** (3), 108–14.
Park, K. (1997) 'Choosing and Using Objects of Reference' *The SLD Experience* **19**, 16–17.
Park, K. (1999/2000) 'Reading Objects: Literacy and Objects of Reference'. *PMLD Link* **12** (1), 4–9.

CHAPTER 9

Delivering the curriculum through drama

Drama for pupils with PMLD

The idea of introducing drama into the curriculum for pupils with PMLD can be very daunting. Staff may feel that they lack training, ideas and inspiration or think that their pupils are not ready for make-believe play. Peter (1994 pp. 13–15) helps to dispel these fears by taking us back to the very beginning of learning about make-believe. She explains that a young baby first discovers pretence through enjoyable turn-taking games with a parent. The baby throws a rattle out of the cot, the adult pretends to be cross and puts it back; the game is repeated over and over again. Peter says that this is the kind of experience that needs to be captured in drama. She proposes that, initially, drama activities will be carefully structured and resemble a game with 'turn-taking, a clearly defined beginning/middle/end and complete in itself'. She lays down pointers for devising drama activities. These include the importance of total involvement by everyone in the group in order to build up a sense of make-believe and 'a shared emotional experience', an atmosphere of tension and a sense of anticipation, and a ritual element controlled by music, rhythm and rhyme. She points out, however, that pupils with physical disabilities or PMLD may startle easily, and the pace will need to be adjusted to avoid sudden shocks. The atmosphere must be fun, relaxed and safe.

The importance of introducing fun into learning has been discussed in previous chapters, and Grove and Park (1996 pp. 69–77) and Peter (1994 p. 15) suggest that drama is a useful tool for delivery of most of the 11 subjects of the curriculum. Grove and Park also offer suggestions for record keeping and describe the part drama can play in developing active and intentional communication.

Drama and inclusion

Learning through doing and having the chance to experience through the senses is important for everyone regardless of age or learning ability. Oily Cart and Interplay are theatre companies specialising in delivering drama to pupils in special schools through whole-sensory experiences. Gardner (1999), reporting in *Theatre First* about the work of Oily Cart says that 'they have discovered what so much other theatre has forgotten – the spoken word is but one way of communicating'. She recognises a huge hunger for audience participation in theatre productions and says that the Oily Cart Company is in advance of mainstream in catering for this. It is true that performances which are interactive and appealing to the senses, such as the circus or pantomime, attract audiences of all ages and from all backgrounds. For these reasons, drama is an excellent medium for inclusive teaching with benefits all round when mainstream and pupils with special needs work together. Extended activities for mainstream pupils could include pupils writing their own 'sensory' stories, helping to adapt literature for the older pupils with PMLD and putting on joint productions. Mencap (1999 p.96) offer further suggestions making story-telling activities suitable for those who need a multisensory approach while extending the intellectual demands of mainstream pupils, and Chapter 6 of this book illustrates what can be done with motivated staff from both schools working together.

Getting started

For anyone feeling inspired to use drama as a teaching medium, some suggestions are offered to help with getting started.

Build on your own ideas – keep it simple

The most important resource for all teachers is their knowledge of their own pupils and their own creative imagination, and for this reason it is important to look first at what can be done with the resources already available. Any ideas for making routine programmes more exciting will help to keep staff interested and alert and may help the pupils to put skills in a context. The theme of the topic or module for the term can be a starting point for introducing a simple dramatic activity into a regular physical programme (see example in Chapter 3). In the same way, activities in the dark room for the teaching of looking, listening and communication skills can be used to create a simple storyline.

Example

Children will be in the classroom in chairs which can be wheeled. Build up an atmosphere of expectation by showing objects of reference to indicate darkroom activities such as a torch shining on holographic paper, and start to play disco music. 'It's Saturday night and we're going to the disco.' All move to dark room.

Time to dress up. Shine torches into boxes and pupils and adults choose an item of clothing in turn – include shiny hats, tinsel wigs, flashing bow ties and sparkly glasses. Shine torch on each pupil in turn and encourage pupils to notice one another.

Turn lights up slowly and put on make-up, earrings, hair gel, perfume and aftershave while looking in mirrors. Look at each other, as above.

Dance time. Turn down lights and turn on spotlight on mirror ball or shine torch on sequined material. Choose a pupil to operate the tape recorder with a timer switch and hold hands and dance. Still when the music stops and wait for it to re-start.

At a suitable time, turn off the spotlight and turn the lights on gradually. Yawning, say slowly, 'It's morning and time to go home' – sing 'goodbye' to each other and leave the room one at a time.

Literature can also help to trigger ideas. Peter (1994 pp. 16, 56–7) gives examples of drama activities built round a bus ride, crossing the road, and a train ride, and these activities could be adapted to recall any outing or visit. The story can be simple and dramatised with readily obtainable props, and a memory box can be compiled with souvenirs from the visit to include sounds, smells and feels which can be incorporated into the story at the appropriate time. The Mencap resource pack, already mentioned, was primarily intended for the families of pupils who need a sensory approach to dramatic story telling, but it is full of ideas which can be used in the classroom.

For teachers with the resources and enthusiasm to take on more ambitious projects, there are adaptations of classical books particularly suitable for older pupils, with suggestions for dramatising the stories through games, music, pictorial slides and a multisensory approach. A list of these materials can be found in the Resources section in Part 2 of this book. More ideas can be found in Fawkes *et al.* (1999), where a collection of case studies and papers illustrate the ways in which teachers have used television, video and computers to support the learning of pupils with SLD and PMLD. One case study describes how a group of pupils aged 12 to 14 were enabled to participate in a performance of as complex a piece of literature as *The Tempest*. Students made a chant on the drum machine to accompany Shakespeare's words in a rap ditty, used switches to operate keyboards, a drum machine and sound effects, and used their own recorded voices to make scary and eerie noises. The final performance was put on video and shown to the rest of the school. There are also examples of using film and video to build up sensory resources to make drama productions more exciting and realistic, such as creating a 'water video' compiled from clips of film with a watery theme. Such a drama production could be made the focus for work over a school term. Another useful resource is *Odyssey Now* (Grove and Park 1996), a dramatisation of the story of

Odysseus through games, music and pictorial slides. Each of the eight instalments of the story is presented as a contained activity and, with the included information about National Curriculum coverage, teachers will find clear material for planning a long-term project.

Themed packages can also offer a good starting point for teachers who are unsure of how to begin with drama. Two such packages, namely *Seaside* and *Galaxies*, among others developed by Consortium (a company which has now folded), are excellent for use with pupils with PMLD, the latter being particularly suitable for older pupils and mainstream children. Although at the time of writing these appear to be out of production, it may be possible to find and borrow existing material.

Invite a professional group into school

There are innovative theatre groups for people with learning disabilities throughout the UK and Europe and some of these specialise in working with small groups of children with PMLD. Groups such as the Oily Cart Theatre Company and the Interplay Theatre offer 'one off' performances which could best be described as sensory voyages of discovery for the children. The level of pupil participation will be to some extent dictated by participating schools, as educational material is provided, and this can be used to plan towards the event, place the day in context and continue the theme afterwards. The Oily Cart *Big Splash* activity pack has suggestions for activities and resources linked to the curriculum and staff may choose to plan the topic for the term around the theme of the production. The setting for 'Big Splash' is a laundry and the school swimming or hydrotherapy pool is turned into an amazing washing world. Sixteen children can be involved during the course of a day, and the performers take them two at a time on a voyage of sensory discovery in search of the 'missing socks'. However schools decide to use the materials, a visit from such a theatre group can turn a dull school hall or swimming pool into a magical setting and the experience will probably never be forgotten by staff or pupils. Teaching methods will certainly be influenced by a visit from such a group!

Other groups offer workshops which run over a period of time. One such organisation is The Ark, whose weekly workshops continue for at least a year, enabling time to develop work of depth. To quote from their literature, they offer multisensory theatre that 'excites all the senses by exploring music making, dance and drama'. Mencap is currently working with the Open Theatre Company to draw up a database and archive of theatre and learning disability work and the Resources section in Part 2 lists groups claiming to provide some service for pupils with PMLD. There are also organisations and independent consultants who will come into schools and work with pupils on multimedia projects. Those involved are usually professional musicians and actors who work alongside staff with the aim of encouraging them to see teaching as a creative activity requiring an imaginative and interactive approach. It is also worth approaching professionals working with the Soundbeam and the resonance board to explore ways in which these can be used to introduce drama into the curriculum. The Resources section in Part 2 has information about individuals and organisations mentioned and others working in this area.

Use of puppets

For most pupils with PMLD, puppets are a great source of fascination. It is often possible to gain attention with a puppet where other methods fail. Some pupils find making eye contact with another person very threatening, but have no problem relating to a puppet. At a simple level, puppets can be home made by painting faces on wooden spoons or plastic bottles, or can be obtained cheaply – 'animal' oven gloves work very well! Pop-up toys are good for catching attention and for helping children to anticipate and understand the concept of object permanence. Shadow puppets have also been used very effectively with pupils with PMLD as the contrast of strong moving objects on a plain background make these particularly good for pupils with limited vision or poor concentration. A dark room with limited distractions is an added bonus, and there is the possibility of introducing coloured lights and sound for a really dramatic performance.

For those who feel enthusiastic about the use of puppets with their pupils and want to explore the subject further, The Puppet Centre periodically raises funds to undertake major educational projects and residencies within schools, particularly in the area of special needs. They will send an education pack on request with hints for making and using puppets and with information as to the role puppetry can play within the National Curriculum. The Resources section in Part 2 has further details about this organisation and of another professional contact for Inset in school. There is also a list of books with ideas for making and using puppets, descriptions of puppets both inexpensive and sophisticated, and information about where they can be obtained.

Suggested further reading

Cattanach, A. (1992) *Drama for People with Special Needs.* London: A. and C. Black (in particular Chapter 9, pp. 126–36, on Drama with Multiply Disabled People).

Leigh, H. (1999/2000) 'Literacy and Drama', *PMLD Link* **12** (1), 24–7.

Longhorn, F. (2000) *Sensory Drama for Very Special Learners.* Wootton, Beds: Catalyst Education Resources.

Peter, M. (1994) – see Bibliography.

CHAPTER 10

Record keeping and assessment

Record keeping could arguably be the most difficult aspect of teaching pupils with PMLD. From experience, problems arise from attempting to keep records which are sufficiently detailed to be useful while being simple enough to ensure delivery, and it is important to decide what to record, when to record, how to record and for whom to record. Each of these issues will be discussed in an attempt to provide guidelines to an efficient and user-friendly system, and a sample record keeping sheet is offered in Part 2 to demonstrate one way in which recording could be managed.

What to record

Meaningful record keeping will be a continuous rather than an occasional process. Teachers who are familiar with the curriculum and the learning targets in each pupil's Individual Education Plan (IEP) will be aware of new and significant responses and ready to take note of these throughout the day. This information will need to be passed on regularly to all adults working with the children – record keeping must be a shared process. Teachers will also need to have a good internalised understanding of the sequence of learning for *all* children, while realising that pupils with PMLD may not follow this sequence in a straight line. This will require flexiblility in what is expected and an absence of preconceived ideas as to the order in which stages will be reached. It is just as important to record the process as it is to record the end result.

For pupils with PMLD, ticks in boxes will never provide the amount of information needed to plan for meaningful teaching and may imply that pupils have not progressed throughout their school life. Provision *must* be made for recording progress as a widening breadth of experience as well as in terms of achievement. Other important facts worth noting are the contexts in which learning has taken place, any motivating factors, and adults working with the child at the time. The latter is important as adults with poor knowledge of a child may interpret behaviour in a different way from someone with whom the pupil has a close relationship.

As already mentioned in Chapter 1, pupils with multiple disabilities may need detailed assessment of their level of functioning in order to plan for their particular needs and strengths. The Suggested further reading section below has suggestions for schemes that can assist with this. Provision may also be needed for recording programmes involving specialist input such as physiotherapy, although study of the documents in Part 2 will reveal that, with a little initiative, it is possible to record most activities under the core subjects.

When to record

Collis and Lacey (1996 p. 107) acknowledge the difficulties faced when trying to run a group and record at the same time. They offer suggestions for making the system work and these are summarised thus:

- give the responsibility to one member of the group;
- make time for assessment during the session;
- record with the pupils after the session;
- make time for staff to get together after the session;
- have regular record-keeping meetings;
- use a simplified method of recording and fill in the details afterwards;
- use another form of recording, e.g. a video camera.

Whatever method teachers decide to use, some important issues are raised. These include the necessity for record keeping to be viewed as a valuable part of teaching, the need for self-discipline and a systematic routine for this to be achieved, and the importance of simplified lesson plans in order to allow time for discussion and assessment. It is all too tempting to try to fit everything into one session, knowing how much has to be covered in a short day, but this way of thinking is always counter productive. It is better to cover a few things properly than to rush through a packed programme. Some suggestions for using a video camera will be discussed later.

How to record

As already discussed, the cross-curricular aspects of teaching pupils with PMLD can create considerable difficulties with recording. One solution is to plan across the range of subjects in order to ensure a broad and balanced curriculum (see Chapter 2) but to record under the core subjects only. However, if teachers wish to make a summative assessment for *all* subjects, this will be possible if learning contexts have been recorded throughout the year. Topic planning gives the opportunity to use photocopied worksheets for the class with space for recording individual responses and evidence of work covered. Priorities highlighted in the pupils' IEPs will need more emphasis and the core subjects of the curriculum should provide for both teaching and goal setting for these targets.

The importance of shared record keeping has already been stressed. One way of achieving this is to provide personal notebooks to accompany each child for noting any significant reactions or achievements – these can be transferred to formal recording sheets at a later date. For close observation of individual pupils over a period of time, a video camera is an excellent tool for recording behaviour which could otherwise be missed in a busy classroom. Ideally, a member of staff can be given the responsibility for using this, but if this is not possible it can be set up in a safe position in the room. Information gained can be used for assessment purposes or for reviewing progress.

For whom to record

Teachers

Aitken and Buultjens (1992 p. 50) say 'evaluation is something that should take place, not of the learner but of one's working practices and methods'. First and foremost, any recording method must supply the information needed to enable teachers to evaluate their professional development and work, take a pupil's learning forward, re-think curriculum planning and report in an informed manner to parents and the wider community. There will be areas of achievement which are difficult to test and the teacher's knowledge of the pupil will always be needed in order to make a rounded judgement, but systematic assessment against standardised attainment targets such as the P Scales must be an important part of the process. Another important aspect of record keeping is to provide continuity for pupils as they progress through the school. With a standardised system of assessment this should be easier, but sufficient detail will be needed in order to paint a true picture of a pupil with PMLD and ensure a smooth transition to a new class.

Pupils

The *Code of Practice on the Identification and Assessment of Special Educational Needs* (DFE,1994) stresses the need to listen to children and young people and to give them the fullest opportunity to have some input into their education and key issues in their life. Initially this may seem to be impossible for pupils with PMLD, but if teaching has been an interactive process and recording has identified likes and dislikes in relation to food, activities, places, people etc. it *will* be possible for them to influence their education. Adults should use the information gained from recording to allow choices, modify or change programmes and write IEPs. Pupils' Records of Achievement (RoA) should reflect their interests as well as their achievements, and with a little imagination photographs and sensory materials can be included which will enable the pupils to have ownership of their own records.

Families and carers

Reporting to family and carers will be an on-going process and as previously suggested this can take place on a daily basis in the form of a home-school diary or recording message device which travels between school and home. It is important to involve the whole family, not only the mother, and imaginative reporting will help to include everyone in the process.

Example

A video and/or class book could be made of work done on the topic for the term and sent home to each family in turn. The book could include photographs, art and craft work, computer print-outs and group work sheets – from experience, parents and grandparents really enjoy borrowing these books or looking at them when they visit school. Siblings can often feel left out and videos and books provide good opportunities for sharing.

Annual reviews can be depressing for parents who have experienced their children regressing physically as they get older. One way of making them a positive experience is to reinforce information in the statement by showing a video of the pupil participating in a wide range of activities with emphasis on things they really enjoy. Parents get real encouragement as they observe their child's involvement in the process of reviewing their provision. Another advantage of a video is that it can be borrowed and shown to family members who were unable to attend the review.

Records of Achievement will be really appreciated by parents if photographs of their children are included. There should always be a space for relatives and carers to add their comments on the records and to say what their child enjoys doing at home, their likes and dislikes, any new achievements and methods of working with them which have proved successful etc.

For wider accreditation

Teachers are accountable to parents, governors and inspectors among others, and will need to be able to prove that their pupils are offered a broad and balanced curriculum. Teachers of pupils with special difficulties will also need to show that their pupils are given the necessary support to access knowledge, skills and understanding at an appropriate and relevant level, with progression encouraged and expected. The Qualifications and Curriculum Authority (QCA) are in the process of revising the Level Descriptions or P Scales (DfEE/QCA 1998) to provide assessment indicators, describe the early learning process and support teachers in understanding where pupils are and how to help them to progress. Lancashire County Council have devised an extended version of the P Scales with Performance Indicators for Value Added Target Setting (PIVATS). Performance indicators are broken down into yet smaller steps, providing a clear means of measuring the attainments of pupils operating below Level 1 in English, mathematics and areas of personal and social development. PIVATS is intended for making baseline and summative assessments and could be used at the same time as standard assessment tasks/tests or at the end of a key stage or before an annual review.

Pupils at the senior end of the school have the same right as their mainstream peers to leave school with some external accreditation. The Award Scheme Development and Accreditation Network (ASDAN) is approved by QCA and offers programmes designed to complement and broaden the school curriculum. Their *Working Towards Independence* programme caters for people over the age of 16 with severe and profound learning difficulties and presents a framework of activities through which personal, social and independent skills can be developed and accredited. Another accreditation scheme designed specifically for pupils with severe or profound learning difficulties is *Accreditation of Life and Living* (ALL). This scheme was developed by a group of teachers who identified the need for customised awards to meet the specific needs of people for whom no suitable national awards existed, and is accredited by the Oxford Cambridge and RSA Examination Board (OCR). Both schemes accredit activities and experiences that are provided within statutory programmes of study for Key Stage 4 of NC subjects and other national initiatives such as the National Education and Training Targets. Centres wishing to run either award must satisfy certain conditions, but teachers and pupils will benefit from carefully devised programmes which will ensure that pupils have the opportunity to practise the skills they have been learning in environments appropriate for their age, and to make a smooth transfer to further education. Further information will be sent on request and contact details can be found in the Useful addresses section in Part 2.

Suggested further reading

Chesworth, S. (1994) 'Devising and Implementing a Cross-Curricular School Recording System' in Rose, R. *et al.* (eds) *Implementing the Whole Curriculum for Pupils with Learning Difficulties*. London: David Fulton Publishers.
Collis, M. and Lacey, P. (1996) – see Bibliography.

Hardwick, J. and Rushton, P. (1994) 'Pupil Participation in their own Record of Achievement', in Rose, R. *et al.* (eds) *Implementing the Whole Curriculum for Pupils with Learning Difficulties.* London: David Fulton Publishers.

Latham, C. and Miles. A. (1996) *Assessing Communication.* London: David Fulton Publishers.

Lawson, H. (1993) *Practical Record Keeping in Special Schools.* London: David Fulton Publishers.

Maskell, S. *et al.* Brown, E. (Ed.) *Baseline Assessment Curriculum and Target Setting for Pupils with Profound and Multiple Learning Difficulties.* London: David Fulton Publishers.

National Curriculum Council (1993) *The National Curriculum and Children with Severe Learning Difficulties.* York: NCC.

Robertson, C. and Cornwall, J. (1999) *IEP's – Learning Difficulties.* London: David Fulton Publishers.

For detailed assessment

Aitken, S. and Buultjens, M. (1992) – see Bibliography.

Coupe, J. *et al.* (1985) *Affective Communication Assessment.* Manchester: Manchester Education Committee.

Kiernan, C. and Reid, B. (1987) – see Bibliography.

Conclusion

Creativity has as much to do with what people know as with what people do. It requires the ability to solve problems progressively over time and apply previous knowledge to new situations. It must be developed through the interaction of the learner, their underlying goals and motivations, and the resources and context in which they operate. Our definition is relatively simple. Creativity is the application of knowledge and skills in new ways to achieve a valued goal. (Bentley 2000 p. 18)

Of all educational institutions, special schools have probably been at the forefront of creative thinking with teachers being left to work out their own curriculum guidelines and to devise effective methods of helping pupils with severe learning difficulties to learn. At long last their needs are being taken seriously and it is accepted that these pupils have as much right as their mainstream peers to a commonly agreed approach to the curriculum with standardised indicators for judging performance. The delivery of the curriculum will always need an imaginative approach, however, and teachers deserve all the help they can get to remain inspired and motivated. Hopefully, this book will have encouraged readers to try something new and given them the confidence to believe that anybody can think creatively when ideas are shared – no particular skill is needed, only the willingness to 'have a go'. Cynthia Heimel (1983) sums up the attitude needed: 'When in doubt, make a fool of yourself. There is a microscopically thin line between being brilliantly creative and acting like the most gigantic idiot on earth. So what the hell, leap'.

Creativity does not take place in a vacuum and it will usually be the result of seeking to solve a problem. Sometimes good ideas come about almost by accident, as is illustrated in the following story. A teacher in a school for pupils with severe learning difficulties was attempting to get the pupils interested in looking at tadpoles – all to no avail. Knowing that his pupils could concentrate better in an environment with few distractions, he took the bowl into the dark room and almost by accident put it down on the overhead projector. Magically, wriggling black shapes were suddenly projected round the room, which immediately fascinated and captivated the attention of the children. This was not an earth shattering revelation, nor did it involve complicated or expensive technology, but this one incident acted as a trigger for a host of other ideas and he was able to transfer what he had discovered to a range of different teaching contexts. As others read about this they are probably thinking of more possibilities, and so creative thinking is fostered. Some of the best ideas are developed when groups of different disciplines get together and share their perspectives and it is often revealing to attend training days run by professionals outside the realm of education. Ideas can also be shared with a wider audience through publications such as *PMLD Link* or on the Internet; teachers of pupils with PMLD are no longer isolated as in the past.

Returning to the image at the beginning of this book of children playing on a beach, we see the value of looking for possibilities for teaching and learning in any situation or environment. Sitting down and actually listing all these possibilities can be an eye-opener to the value of taking a sensory approach to teaching the curriculum to all pupils, and especially to those with profound and complex learning needs. The building blocks for planning this approach will be a good knowledge of what has to be taught and an understanding of the particular learning needs of individual children. Once these are in place it will be possible to make teaching and learning enjoyable for both staff and pupils. Being willing to experiment may result in some failures, but never in boredom.

Although we can all be encouraged to think more imaginatively, there are some to whom this comes more naturally than others. These people are creative artists in their own fields, and observing them in action can be a real inspiration as they are not afraid to take risks or look foolish. We cannot all have their gifts of spontaneous and uninhibited creativity but some of this can be absorbed when working together on a project. This is discussed further in Chapter 9 and there are names in the Resources section in the Part 2 of this book of individuals and organisations with expertise in working with pupils with PMLD. It is strongly recommended that schools take advantage of their gifts for one-off events or for long-term projects.

The past decade has been one of radical change in the education of pupils with PMLD: technology allows them to play a more active part in classroom activities and opens up new means of communicating; there are more opportunities for them to be included with their peer group and to be part of the community; curriculum needs are at last being taken seriously and their right to the same curriculum as pupils in mainstream is now acknowledged. However, change for its own sake is meaningless and it is all too easy to throw out the old methods and mindlessly adopt the new. Teachers must be very clear about their goals and be willing to try new ways of achieving them, but at the same time must constantly evaluate what works best for their own pupils. It would be sad if the particular qualities special schools have to offer are lost as integration gains momentum. It would be good to think that a sensitive, imaginative and sensory approach to teaching could be taken up by mainstream staff with benefits for all pupils.

Taylor and Hallgarten (2000 pp. 9–10), speaking of recent curriculum changes, say that we need to be alert to the fact that what was previously known as a 'secret garden' may be in danger of becoming an 'overmanicured lawn'. Teachers must never lose sight of the fact that teaching is an art and they must resist all attempts to stifle instincts and inspiration. A secret garden conjures up the idea of spontaneity, delight and constant surprises and *all* pupils need such an environment if they are to thrive and grow.

PART 2

Curriculum document and sample record keeping sheet

A sensory approach to English, mathematics and science in the curriculum

Using the curriculum document

The main aim of this document is to interpret what the Attainment Targets in the core subjects of the National Curriculum mean to pupils with profound and multiple learning difficulties, and to give suggestions for activities and teaching strategies to help them work towards and achieve those targets. It would not be possible or desirable to produce a fully comprehensive document since teachers will have their own ideas, but the following uses are suggested:

- to provide access to the mainstream curriculum for pupils with PMLD;
- to give insight to mainstream staff as to the appropriate teaching levels for pupils with PMLD;
- as a curriculum in its own right;
- as a resource to complement an existing school curriculum;
- as an aid to imaginative teaching.

Some pupils may need to work at grasping basic skills and concepts throughout their lives but this does not mean that they have to work at a childish level. Teachers should choose suggested activities to suit the age of their pupils and build in progression through a widening range of learning environments. Identified learning targets *must* relate closely to the programmes of study followed, and constant cross-referencing from one to the other will provide a reason for each activity and a means of helping pupils to reach their individual targets. There should be the opportunity to record progress both in terms of breadth of experience and achievement. One suggestion for record keeping can be found at the end of the curriculum document.

Details about materials mentioned in this document are to be found in the Resources section, and addresses of suppliers are also listed there. Books are listed in the Bibliography.

English   Speaking and Listening

Objective	POS	Suggested Activities/Strategies	Suggested Resources
National Curriculum (NC) AT 1 Level 1 Pupils talk about matters of immediate interest	Pupils should be given opportunities to: participate in programmes and activities designed to develop the skills of sucking, chewing, licking, swallowing, lip closure and breath control necessary for the acquisition of speech;	Facial massage, blowing practice. Amplify and focus on their sounds (breathing, sucking, chewing, licking) and play with these sounds (as in *Beat That!/Soundabout*). Allow pupils to smell and see food before eating. Mash or chop foods separately. Offer a wide range of tastes, consistencies and textures. Introduce new tastes and textures slowly, preferably at the start of a meal when the pupil is hungry. Where appropriate, pupils can practise dipping fingers in food and licking it off. NB For children with eating difficulties a speech and language therapist should be consulted as to a suitable feeding programme. The school physiotherapist will advise on the correct position for head support in order to achieve mouth control.	Meal times Cookery sessions – give opportunities to cook their own lunch Tasting sessions Multicultural celebrations Suitable objects to mouth Objects to blow such as tinsel, tissue paper and candles Breath control games in Halliwick swimming sessions and physical programmes *Beat That!/Soundabout* activities For further guidelines see: *The Stimulation Guide* (Dale 1990) pp. 124–31 *The Practical Management of Eating and Drinking Difficulties in Children* (Winstock 1994). This and other books on feeding and swallowing can be obtained from Winslow.
National Literacy Strategy (NLS) Vocabulary extension **Personal and Social Development (PSD)** Independent and organisational skills	learn the basic skills needed for an understanding of their immediate environment.	Pupils should follow carefully structured programmes in a room with limited distractions in order to learn skills of looking, fixating, tracking, listening, noticing themselves and others. Opportunities will arise throughout the day to practise these skills in context and in a widening range of environments.	Darkened room with visually/auditory stimulating materials and a source of light. See: TFH catalogue for a range of materials and equipment for a dark room; Stocking fillas catalogue and local shops for inexpensive items; *Fun and Games* Denziloe (1994) pp. 29–40 for ideas for activities; Longhorn (1997) on the use of ultraviolet light and fluorescing materials.

English   Speaking and Listening

Objective	POS	Suggested Activities/Strategies	Suggested Resources
NC AT 1 Level 1 Pupils talk about matters of immediate interest **NLS** Vocabulary extension **PSD** Interacting and working with others Independent and organisational skills Attention	Pupils should be given opportunities to: discover how the body moves;	See activities and resources on Maths pp. 76, 85 and Science p. 89, and resources in next section. Group sessions round a resonance board – leader mirrors a pupil's movement and augments it (e.g. Beat That, Soundabout). Sherborne movement, swimming etc. Experience vibration on parts of the body (see Denziloe 1994 pp. 48–9).	Hang attractive objects for children to knock with parts of the body – ideas for making mobiles can be found in *Fun and Games* (Denziloe 1994) pp24–28). Hang everyday objects with visual or sound making properties or interesting textures.
	use body language to communicate basic needs and emotions;	Give pupils a need to communicate. Value all behaviours as communicative and respond positively (see *Creating a Responsive Environment* Ware 1996).	Use an assessment schedule to interpret behaviours (see Suggested reading, Chapter 10). Use a video camera for detailed observation.
	acquire a sound self-image and an awareness of self in relation to others;	Observe consistent responses and record. Use focused activities in a dark room to encourage pupils to notice others in the group. Play games which involve shining a torch on pupils in turn e.g. musical hats with shiny hat or tinsel wig, dressing up, making up, waving shiny or fluorescent toys. Celebrate special events such as birthdays, religious and cultural festivals, and personal achievements.	Encourage looking at self and others with: tinsel wigs, shiny clothes, face paints, nail polish, earrings See Longhorn (1997) for a resource tpack on he use of fluorescing materials (details in Chapter 2). For encouraging general 'looking skills see Early Years and Sensory Software – available from SEMERC.
	interact with others.	Play one to one games between adult and pupil e.g. looking in the mirror, peep-bo, pulling silly hats off each other's heads, imitating funny faces, noises and actions, rolling balls or toys to each other. Use pleasurable activities to bond relationships such as aromatherapy massage and *Tac Pac.*	See: *Fun and Games* Denziloe 1994 pp. 110–13 for an exciting collection of balls and for ideas for turn-taking games; TFH catalogue for toys and equipment; *Fun and Games* Denziloe 1994 pp. 51–63 for aromatherapy massage; suggested activities for Maths p. 79.

English   Speaking and Listening

Objective	POS	Suggested Activities/Strategies	Suggested Resources
NC AT1 Level 1 They listen to others and usually respond appropriately	Pupils should be given opportunities to: locate and track sounds;	Go round the group with a musical instrument. Play instrument behind a screen. Roll a noisy toy across the floor. Use IT programs (see Resources column).	Musical instruments Balls containing bells/wobble ball Battery toys Sound panels in sensory room IT programs such as *Look here* (Sensory software from Inclusive Technology) (see *Fun and Games* Denziloe 1994 pp. 38–40)
NLS Phonological awareness Phonics and spelling Vocabulary extension	listen attentively to an adult;	Attract interest by wearing an eye-catching hat, wig or glasses.	Fluorescent and shiny materials in dark room Makaton signing An introduction card with child's name and photo to encourage others to interact Resonance board
	respond to the sound of their own name;	Come close to child, speak clearly using name and wait for eye contact or other sign of response before continuing the conversation. Use signing to reinforce speech. Gain attention by talking 'through' a puppet. Play name games as on English p. 73.	
PSD Interacting and working with others	experience and enjoy vocalising;	Encourage vocalisation by the following: amplify any sounds made by use of a microphone, Zube tube, megaphone etc; create music round a child's sounds; create silences for pupils to put in their own sounds as in Beat That and Soundabout activities; offer sound-activated equipment and toys; record pupil's sounds and play back;	ICT programs such as *Speak up* (Sensory software from Inclusive Tech.) Splatter 2 (new Sensory Software from SEMERC) Microphone Zube tube Micro Mike Megaphone Equipment in dark room which responds to sound Sound activated toys Tape recorder
	vocalise with an intent to communicate.	respond to any vocalisation and talk back; keep a record of times when pupil is most vocal; record different sounds made; build a picture of intended meaning. NB Consult the speech therapist as to programmes for stimulating facial muscles.	(see TFH catalogue)

English   Speaking and Listening

Objective	POS	Suggested Activities/Strategies	Suggested Resources
NC AT1 Level 1 They convey simple meanings to a range of listeners and begin to extend their ideas or accounts by providing some detail	Pupils should be given opportunities to: work with interactive toys and equipment which will encourage more complex and intentional actions on the environment;	Pupils to use switches with: sound-making toys, percussion instruments, tape recorder and radio, IT software; kitchen equipment such as food mixer, liquidiser; household or office equipment such as washing machine, vacuum cleaner, photocopier.	Switch toys (see Resources and TFH) Tape recorder, radio Musical instruments Food mixer, liquidiser, vacuum cleaner, photocopier (Place on resonance board where suitable to amplify sound.)
NLS Vocabulary extension Understanding of print	activate and listen to speech and a range of sounds through ICT programs;	Computer programs producing sound and colour e.g. *Build it* (Sensory software from Inclusive Technology). *SwitchOn* actions/travel/zoo and *Touch games 1 and 2* (SEMERC). For unusual and motivating switches see TFH (see also Figures 8.3 and 8.4 in Chapter 8).	Pethna box (TFH catalogue) Touch screen Switch programs Concept keyboard Intercom system Sound activated toys Sound switch microphone (TFH)
PSD Interacting and working with others Independent and organisational skills Attention	discover a variety of ways to express choices, needs or preferences.	Always offer a choice – food is a good starting point. Start by offering: ● the real thing ● partial or associated object ● photograph of object ● line drawing (symbol) of object. If pupils recognise the photo or symbolic representation this can be attached to an E Tran Frame or a switch. Pupils can look at the object or symbolic representation to communicate needs, or touch the switch to activate a recorded message. Always reinforce speech with signing.	Personal communication books Aids to communication to include: ETran Frame, Echo 4, BIGmac; touch screen programs; concept keyboard; sets of professional photographs (Winslow); magazine photographs; Rebus symbols or PCS; Makaton signing. (For stockists and further ideas see the Resources list.)

English   Reading

Objective	POS	Suggested Activities/Strategies	Suggested Resources
NC AT2 Level 1 Pupils recognise familiar words in simple texts	Pupils should be given opportunities to: understand the link between an object and its pictorial or symbolic representation;	Use real objects alongside pictures in storytelling. Have symbols on objects or activities around room. Make personalised objects of reference to inform of activities – these must be consistent and personal to pupil. (see also English p. 71, Maths p. 82, and Chapter 8).	A variety of familiar objects to explore Clear pictures and photos of objects Magazines Rebus symbols/PCS Story sacks Tactile story boards or home made equivalent Symbol software (see Resources section and Suppliers addresess)
NLS Word recognition	recognise photographs of themselves and familiar people;	Make photo albums and videos of children at home. Show photos alongside other clues such as parent or siblings' voices, mum's perfume, dad's aftershave or tobacco, or associated sounds of people working in school such as kitchen noises or photocopier.	
Vocabulary extension			
Understanding of print			
Reading comprehension	use their knowledge of visual clues to understand and recall activities and events.	Make videos of outings and books with large print photos and symbols. Add textures, sounds and smells where appropriate to reinforce recall. Make books about regular walks to the shops and include food packaging and smells, textures touched on route such as a hedge or brick wall, real objects such as money and sweets (stuck down).	Photograph albums/plastic wallets Scrap books Book-making equipment, e.g. laminator and binder (see Fuller 1990) Camera, video camera, tape recorder, digital camera, digitiser for computer Set of social signs
Composition			
PSD Independent and organisational skills		Make books about regular food preparation activities such as making a cup of tea or toast. Include photos, symbols, smells (e.g. a real tea bag) and listen to accompanying sounds such as water running, spoon stirring, toast popping up. Make recipe books of special cooking – e.g. a Christmas cake or chutney. Sprinkle ingredients such as raisins, sugar and spices onto glued pages.	Cooking ingredients Cooking utensils Commercial books with sounds Sound lotto game: Human/daily/home/transport/animal sounds (see Winslow catalogue) Rebus symbols or similar system
Attention			

English   Reading

Objective	POS	Suggested Activities/Strategies	Suggested Resources
NC AT2 Level 1 Pupils use their knowledge of letters and sound–symbol relationships in order to read words and to establish meaning when reading aloud. In these activities they sometimes require support	Pupils should be given opportunities to: listen to and enjoy the sounds letters make;	Make sounds on pupil's body and whisper in ear. Encourage pupils to watch mouth movements and imitate – mirrors can be helpful. Listen to alliteration, sound pattern and rhyme. Use puppets with moveable mouths (see Resources section)	Mirrors Music therapy sessions Sessions round the resonance board Puppets (see Resources section)
NLS Phonological awareness		Use games round a resonance board to have fun with different sounds, for example: Start a simple beat. Caller chants a pupil's name to this beat and this is taken up by next adult who extends and accentuates the vowel sounds.	Contact Beat That! and Soundabout for further information about games round a resonance board and 'name' games (see Resources section)
Phonics and spelling	be helped to make a link between the initial letter of their first name and themselves.	Make large tactile initials and use at roll call, music sessions and in Motor Education Programmes – pupils can be helped to feel the outline of their initial with their fingers. Draw initial in sand, finger paints, cornflour and water etc. Roll out in clay, play dough.	Large tactile and visually attractive initials Wet and dry sand Clay, paints and other tactile, slimy materials
Word recognition			
Vocabulary extension		Draw initials in the air in dark room with Painting the Air (TFH) a wand that produces an amazing trail of light when waved in a darkened room.	
Understanding of print			
Reading comprehension		Play 'name' games, for example: drum pattern of pupils' names and help them to recognise their own; sound initial name consonant e.g. bbbbbbb . . . rise to crescendo . . . BRIAN!	Name games (contact Beat That! and Soundabout as above)
PSD Attention			

English　Reading

Objective	POS	Suggested Activities/Strategies	Suggested Resources
NC AT2 Level 1 They express their response to poems, stories and non-fiction by identifying aspects they like	Pupils should be given opportunities to: explore books by involving as many senses as possible;	Provide a range of sensory materials and record the aspects which most interest individual children. Make books for individual children where possible. Use props when telling stories (see resources in next column and Figures 8.1 and 8.2, in Chapter 8). Sign for familiar words.	Bag Books, story sacks, story boards (for description of Bag Books and other resources see Figure 8.2) Tactile and shiny books (see previous page) Pop-up books Sound-making books Big books
NLS Phonological awareness Phonics and spelling Word recognition Vocabulary extension Understanding of print Reading comprehension	enjoy and participate in storytelling, poetry reading and drama;	Use action songs and rhymes with a strong rhythm. Involve pupils with story telling by recording repetitive phrases in stories on a simple message system such as BIGmack – pupils can take turns to join in. Use puppet play. Use a resonance board to make sounds in stories more dramatic. Drama activities within school – (obtain adapted storytelling material as identified in the Resources section). Visits from theatre companies (see Resources section). Outings to theatre, cinema, circus.	Books of Nursery Rhymes Nonsense rhymes For older pupils, Roald Dahl's *Revolting Rhymes* or limericks (try inventing ones about each other) Story/Symbol pack (Call Centre) Puppets – string and shadow Glove puppets – use socks, oven gloves etc. (see Resources section) Sensory drama packs such as Galaxies and Seaside (no longer available but worth borrowing if they can be found) Odyssey Now
PSD Attention	gain access to further elements of literacy.	See Chapter 8 and in particular Figures 8.3 and 8.4 for suggestions for technology and software to aid pupils to gain access to further elements of literacy.	Early learning computer software CD ROM e.g. Living Books series or various talking stories – especially useful for older pupils (See Resources section for producers and stockists)

English   Writing

Objective	POS	Suggested Activities/Strategies	Suggested Resources
NC AT3 Level 1 Pupils' writing communicates meaning through simple words and phrases Letters are usually clearly shaped and correctly orientated	Pupils should have opportunities to: experience and participate in making marks on surfaces;	NB Ensure pupils are in a good, supported position. Provide a variety of substances for pupils to enjoy feeling and to move their hands and fingers through, e.g. paint, wet clay, wet and dry sand, flour and water paste. Provide materials such as clay and dough for pupils to poke and press with fingers/implements. Finger painting – take prints off. Marbles dipped in paint and rolled on paper. Hand and foot prints. Sponge, vegetable and fruit prints on paper and material, working from left to right. Prints in wet clay. Making marks on Super scribbler or Magic drawing board with implements, stamps or fingers (ELC). Hand impressions on Lumiglow panel (TFH). Tie dying, marbling. 'Drawing' on resonance board – listen to sound shapes – circles, lines, dots, zig-zags. Painting in the air in the dark with Painting the Air (TfH catalogue).	Paint Clay Sand – wet and dry Flour and water paste Cornflour and water paste Jelly Salt dough Variety of objects for printing Sponges Material Dyes Resonance board (For further ideas see *Fun and Games* Denziloe 1994 Chapter 3.)
NLS Hand writing	produce work and begin to show an awareness that they are creating it.	Use computer with touch screen to produce patterns, download, and print out. *Writing with Symbols* programs for pupils for whom this is appropriate. Use pupils' work for displays, cards, presents, book covers, classroom books, invitations etc.	Computer programs from SEMERC Sensory software *(Build it! – Patterns)* *(Kaleidoscope 2)* *(Look Some More)* See Suppliers addresses section in Resources for obtaining catalogues.

Mathematics   Using and Applying Mathematics

Objective	POS	Suggested Activities/Strategies	Suggested Resources
NC AT1 Level 1 Pupils use mathematics as an integral part of class activities. They represent their work with objects or pictures and discuss it. They recognise and use a simple pattern or relationship.	Pupils should be given opportunities to: benefit from an environment which will respond to random movements;	Provide easily accessible materials which will crackle, rattle, shine, tinkle, clatter, bang when touched. Put things that will clatter on the resonance board such as keys, coins and buttons (where safe). Place materials for pupils to kick or roll onto which will provide sensory stimulation. Provide toys and equipment which pupils can activate to produce a sensory effect. Use IT programs, switch toys and other switch activated equipment. (See Resources and Suppliers section for information about suggested equipment.)	Hanging mobiles and chimes Little room of Lillie Neilsen Survival blanket Cellophane paper Bubble pack Tinsel, foil curtain Marbles and shells Resonance board Vibrating floor pad (TFH) Sound beam Touch screen Switch access software Switch toys Vibrating toys and equipment (TFH) Touch sensitive lights and light equipment (TFH)
Framework for teaching mathematics Key objective: Use developing mathematical ideas and methods to solve practical problems.	practise relating objects to their proper function;	Use mirrors when washing, combing hair, brushing teeth, eating and drinking, putting on clothes. Allow time for pupils to feel, smell, listen, look handle and taste, where appropriate in: • cooking, preparing drinks and washing up • household and cleaning tasks • gardening • shopping (money handled under supervision).	Flannels, soap, comb, toothbrush, toothpaste, clothes, mirrors Cup, cutlery, kettle, squash bottles Milk carton Cooking utensils and equipment Garden tools Shopping bags Money
	recognise their own belongings.	Always give pupils the time to indicate their own belongings by eye pointing, touching or grabbing, going towards own peg etc.	Break time, dressing and personal care activities, home time

Mathematics   Using and Applying Mathematics

Objective	POS	Suggested Activities/Strategies	Suggested Resources
AT1 Level 1 (cont) Pupils use mathematics as an integral part of class activities . . . They recognise and use a simple pattern or relationship.	Pupils should be given opportunities to: explore a variety of random and structured materials, both man-made and natural and be helped to notice differences;	Use activities and resources suggested throughout the curriculum to encourage pupils to explore objects and materials with opposite qualities such as rough/ smooth, hard/soft, shiny/dull, heavy/light. Activities may be planned around the topic for the term and built into Motor Education Programmes and Hand Group activities. Listen to sounds made by different materials: Loud, soft, high, low, dull, sharp, crackling, grating.	School topic for the term Planned outings and activities around the topic, e.g. to seaside, ice rink, car factory, bakery Art and craft activities, e.g. collage, using a variety of materials and textured papers, scissors, glue, glitter, sand, and water play (see *Fun and Games* Denziloe 1994 Chapter 7 for ideas for objects to handle) Swimming – hot atmosphere/cool water
Framework for teaching mathematics Key objective: Use developing mathematical ideas and methods to solve practical problems.	explore sets of objects with properties in common;	Place 'like' things where pupils can explore them Hang 'like' things up for pupils to reach. Examples: *All* brushes *All* containers *All* necklaces *All* spoons *All* balls *All* shoes *All* gloves *All* bells *All* spiky *All* cars *All* metal *All* wood *All* flowers *All* shiny Listen to similarities in sound made by like materials. Use a resonance board to accentuate the sounds.	Nature outings to collect natural objects such as fir cones, pebbles, leaves, flowers, twigs Feely bags Little House of Lillie Nielsen Large cardboard box for pupils to lie in – hang things from roof Waldon style teaching – putting or spooning objects in and out of containers
	use equipment in a range of Key Stage appropriate settings.	Information gained about the properties of materials and objects should be reinforced through practical activities involving the use of tools. Pupils should be helped to use the correct tools for the task.	Cookery – raw ingredients/cooked food, cooking utensils Gardening – wet and dry soil, tools for different activities Technology – use of hammer, saw, wood, metal etc.

Mathematics   Number and Algebra

Objective	POS	Suggested Activities/Strategies	Suggested Resources
NC AT2 Level 1 Pupils count, order add and subtract numbers when solving problems involving up to 10 objects. They read and write the numbers involved.	Pupils should have opportunities to: experience and develop awareness of rote counting;	Counting pupils at registration. Counting songs and rhymes. Counting fingers and toes. Counting when dressing, e.g. 2 gloves, 2 socks, 2 shoes. Movement with an adult – count claps, stamps, nods. Play 'fun with numbers' games on the resonance board to include African drumming (contact Beat That!). Counting while putting objects in and out of containers. Birthday cards with large numbers – shiny and colourful or tactile. Count candles on birthday cakes and number of blows. Clap/give the bumps on birthdays.	Song books Music sessions Finger and counting rhymes Nursery rhymes Rap music Reading books Candles Birthday cards All-turn-it spinner for group number games (from Liberator) Waldon style teaching
Framework for teaching mathematics Key objectives: • Say and use number names in familiar contexts. • Count reliably up to 10 everyday objects. • Recognise numerals 1 to 9. • In practical activities, begin to use the vocabulary involved in adding and subtraction. • Find one more or one less than a number 1 to 10.	experience and develop awareness of the difference between one and lots.	Adding and subtracting activities: pupils to experience being part of a small group and a larger group; play musical counting games where children join in one by one; play games such as musical statues where children are eliminated one by one; group sessions around resonance board, e.g. join in with tapping one by one and stopping in turn; percussion sessions – one takes the lead, then all join in. Stop playing in turn. Hand round plate of biscuits etc. – take one at a time	Class groups Whole-school activities Musical games such as: 'Who will join in with my small ring?' 'The farmer's in his den' 'One elephant went out to play' Musical bumps Musical statues

Mathematics   Number and Alegbra

Objective	POS	Suggested Activities/Strategies	Suggested Resources
Framework for teaching mathematics	Pupils should be given opportunities to: repeat an action or sound spontaneously;	Adults to recognise any spontaneous action and respond enthusiastically. Pupil to be encouraged to repeat this action.	Suspended mobiles Little room of Lillie Nielsen Computer touch screen Survival blanket Switched and other interactive toys and equipment Touch sensitive equipment Sound beam Resonance board
Key objective: Talk about, recognise and recreate simple patterns.	establish a pattern of mutual interaction with an adult;	Establish favourite turn-taking activities and make these times of fun and enjoyment, for example: Repeat back babble or facial expression. Do silly actions which create a response, e.g. jumping up and down and waving arms in the air. Wait for sign from pupil to request repeat of action.	
	experience and become aware of repeating patterns and sounds.	Sessions on the resonance board – hold silence and wait for response. Create a sequence using the pupils' own actions or sounds (as in Beat That! and Soundabout activities). Shout into Zube tube, microphone or Karaoke machine – give to pupil to repeat the sound. Participate in African drumming sessions. Experience rhythms on the resonance board. Count actions out loud such as: Clap clap-stamp stamp, clap clap-stamp stamp. Repeat sounds using the Soundbeam. Work Waldon style with pupils, working from left to right, threading alternate coloured beads, building with alternate coloured bricks, printing repeating patterns.	Musical instruments Zube tube Karaoke machine Microphone Colourful, shiny balls Chime ball Wobble ball Toy cars (See *Fun and Games* Denziloe 1994 pp. 110–13 for exciting collection of balls and ideas for turn-taking games.) Percussion instruments Resonance board Coloured blocks, beads, beakers Natural objects, fruit, vegetables and sponges for printing

Mathematics   Shape, Space and Measure

Objective	POS	Suggested Activities/Strategies	Suggested Resources
NC AT3 Level 1 When working with 3D and 2D shapes, pupils use everyday language to describe properties and positions. **Framework for teaching mathematics** Key objective: Use everyday words to describe position.	Pupils should be given opportunities to: experience and develop awareness of object permanence;	Activities in a dark room to encourage pupils to track a moving light. Watching a moving ball or toy – use balls with bells inside, shiny/fluorescent colours, flashing lights. Tracking a moving sound such as a switch toy. Tracking adult with guitar in group situation. Hiding biscuits or sweets under container. Hiding glove puppet behind back – where is it? Use of pop-up books and puppets. Use of computer programs, videos or CD ROM which involve tracking a light or object across screen or watching for an animal or person to appear (see Resources section for suppliers).	Dark room Torches Fibre optic torches, Light rope Glitter poles (see TFH) Sparkly windmills Glitter hats and tinsel wigs Candles Glove and pop-up puppets Touch screen programs such as: *Where's Blob?* (Blob for Windows from Widgit) Hello visual stimulation video (RNIB) CD ROM – Living books (Broderbind/REH)
	use their whole bodies to experience and show awareness of different shapes, sizes and changes of movement and position.	Use a ball pool/soft play area/swimming pool activities/large PE equipment to allow pupils to experience the properties of different 3D shapes and to experience changes of position with their whole body – up/down, above/below, over/under, high/low, behind/in front. Use mathematical vocabulary. Movement sessions with adults to assist pupils to lift arms up and down, roll over, curl up/stretch. Listening to their movements on a resonance board. Noticing who is sitting next to them in the group. **NB** Always inform pupils before a change of position and use consistent language to describe actions and positions.	Soft play area and ball pool Physio ball Slide, swing Play tunnels Large cardboard boxes Parachute games (see *Fun and Games* Denziloe 1994 pp. 116–18) *Listen and Do* (LDA) *Move and Relax with Music* (LDA) Music and resonance board sessions Halliwick swimming programmes Lifting hoist *Tac Pac* *All join in!*, *Sound Moves* (RNIB)

Mathematics   Shape, Space and Measure

Objective	POS	Suggested Activities/Strategies	Suggested Resources
NC AT3 Level 1 They measure and order objects using direct comparison and order events (continues over).	Pupils should be given opportunites to: experience and show awareness of objects placed on their hands or bodies;	Give opportunities for pupils to handle a variety of 3D shapes: ● balls of different sizes ● blocks of different shapes and sizes ● quoits and cones ● help pupils to sort shapes, stack containers and fit shapes (see *Fun and Games* Denziloe 1994 pp. 96–100).	Large and colourful shapes in soft play area, ball pool Small PE equipment in various sizes and shapes Cardboard boxes and tubes Sorting boxes – try using tins with shapes cut out of plastic lids Stacking containers/inset shapes Full and empty containers Balloons filled with sand/water/air Different sizes and weights of balls Sand and water play
Framework for teaching mathematics Key objective: Use language such as circle or bigger to describe the shape and size of solids and flat shapes.	reinforce concepts of shape, size and weight in a range of learning situations;	Plan teaching of these concepts around the topic of the term and build into activities such as: ● hands group exercise programme ● physical programmes ● cookery sessions ● gardening activities ● shopping expeditions.	Cooking ingredients such as bags of flour, sugar, packets of tea Weights Gardening tools Full and empty flower pots Cans and cartons of food
	notice changes in sound – volume, pitch, organised or chaotic, thick or thin, short or long.	Activities on the resonance board using stopping and starting, sound and silence, rhythm, pitch and volume. Create silence for pupils to listen to their own and each other's sounds (*Beat That!* and *Soundabout* activities). Listening to music and taking part. Creating sounds with the Sound beam.	Resonance board Musical instruments and Sound beam

Mathematics   Shape, Space and Measure

Objective	POS	Suggested Activities/Strategies	Suggested Resources
NC AT3 Level 1 (continued from previous page) They measure and order objects using direct comparison and order events.	Pupils should be given opportunities to: notice features in their immediate environment and develop an awareness of different artificial and natural environments;	Different rooms in the school can be identified by sounds, sights and smells, for example: ● sound of photocopier in office ● toilet flushing and water running in bathroom ● lack of light in darkroom ● smells and sounds of cooking in dining room ● chlorine smell, warmth and echoing sounds in swimming pool. Visit places with distinguishing sensory features (see resource list).	Suggested visits to: Swimming pool Train station Bakery Zoo – smell of animals, change of temperature in reptile house, darkness of bat house Ice rink Tropical greenhouse
	build up a picture of a school day and anticipate the order of events.	Use objects of reference to inform pupils of the next event, for example: ● marmite smell + spoon = dinner ● feel and smell of towel = swimming ● torch on reflective paper = darkroom activities ● purse and rattling money = shopping ● sound of bells = music ● smell of lavender oil = massage Use objects of reference when talking through the timetable for the day or, when appropriate, for offering choices to pupils. Use rhythm to talk through daily activities, e.g. Mon-day, swim-ming (Beat That! timetable game). Take note of any body movements or sounds which could indicate anticipation or understanding of where they are (see also Science p. 84).	For more information about objects of reference, tactile calendars and sensory timetables see: Paperback articles by Ockelford and Bloom in the RNIB catalogue *Vision for Doing* (Aitken and Buultjens 1992) pp. 119, 101–6, 160 NB Some objects of reference will be personal for individual pupils, but objects or sounds for timetabled activities may be shared by the whole group and should be used consistently both in the classroom and in other environments.

Science   Scientific Enquiry

Objective	POS	Suggested Activities/Strategies	Suggested Resources
NC AT1 Level 1 Pupils describe and respond appropriately to simple features of objects, living things and events they observe (continues over).	Pupils should have opportunities to: smell, taste, look, listen and feel in order to be able to build up a picture of materials and events.	Pupils should be offered a range of sensory experiences during daily school activities and in planned, structured sessions in a distraction-free environment. Skills learned should be practised in a widening range of age-appropriate environments such as whole-school events, in the locality and in the wider community. Pupils should have opportunities to experience and respond to the senses of: **Taste** Main tastes – salt, sweet, sour, bitter. Subsidiary tastes – fruity, fiery, spicy, bland, herbal, savoury, dried. Consistency and texture – sticky, creamy, fizzy, smooth, coarse, lumpy, thick, liquid. Offer 'hot' and cold food. (See *Sensory Cookery for Very Special People* by Flo Longhorn details in Chapter 2.) **Smell** Pleasant/unpleasant, human/domestic, locational smells, perfumes, medicinal, spicy, household, bathroom, cleaning, herbal, male/female. **Feel** Messy, sticky, slimy, scratchy, rough, smooth, squashy, wet, dry, hot, cold, hard, soft, warm and cold air on skin, touch on skin, vibration. (continues over)	**Taste** (consult speech therapist) School dinners and tasting sessions Variety of drinks to include sweet, savoury, fizzy, thick, thin Unusual and spicy tastes and smells at religious and cultural celebrations **Smell** Incense sticks and scented candles Church smells Kitchen and bathroom smells Laundry smells Herb and flower gardens, cut grass Cookery and washing up activities, cleaning materials – polish, room spray Personal hygiene – soap, deodorant, talcum powder, bubble bath, after-shave, perfume, massage oil Outings to: Body shop, Neals Yard, Culpeppers, Indian restaurant, bakery, coffee shops, florist **Feel** Clay, paint, sand, water, mud, dough, honey, mashed banana, jelly, ice cream, shaving foam, toothpaste, slime, squashy balls, play dough, nail brush, toothbrush, sandpaper, glass, metal, ice, feathers, velvet, fan, wind, footspa, hairdryer, vibrating toys and household appliances, massage

Science   Scientific Enquiry

Objective	POS	Suggested Activities/Strategies	Suggested Resources
NC AT1 Level 1 (continued from previous page) Pupils describe simple features of objects, living things and events they observe, communicating their findings in simple ways.	Pupils should be given opportunities to: smell, taste, look, listen and feel in order to be able to build up a picture of materials and events;	**Look at** Light, dark, flashing light, shadows, patterns, reflections, colours, transparent things, shiny things, movement. **Listen to** Loud, soft, harsh, vibratory, percussion, whistles, wood, brass, squealers, paper noises, mechanical, blowing. Use a resonance board to enhance sounds and combine music with flashing lights to emphasise movement.	**Look at** Dark room equipment both large and small – torches, electric lights, fireworks, candles, reflective materials, mirrors, cellophane, glass in different colours, glass paints, dye, food colouring, computer programs, light toys. Ultra violet light and fluorescent toys and materials (see Longhorn 1997a and TFH catalogue). **Listen to** Percussion instruments Woodwork sounds – saw, hammer, sandpaper, drill Resonance board Hairdryer Jacuzzi and foot spa Weather sounds, traffic sounds, transport sounds, human and animal sounds Machine noises in home, school, office, factory, garden Brass bands and concerts Discos
	integrate sensory input to aid understanding of objects, to make sense of events and assist recall;	**Understand** Pupils can feel and smell objects, listen to sounds made and link to photo or picture. Everyday activities such as tea making, washing up, cleaning and woodwork can be seen as opportunities for multisensory experiences. Visits can be made to places in the wider environment with their own particular sounds and smells. Tape recordings can be made and replayed back at school while looking at large, clear photos of the visit and remembering smells or textures as appropriate.	Visits to supermarkets, zoos, garden centres, factories, discos, ice rink, bowling alley, rail station
	communicate understanding of features of living things and events.	Note reactions and build up a picture of communications, e.g: mouth movements, changes in body movement, startle reactions, vocalisation, standing up, walking to the door etc. Use video camera, assessment schedules. Refer to P Scales.	

Science   Life Processes and Living Things

Objective	POS	Suggested Activities/Strategies	Suggested Resources
NC AT2 Level 1 Pupils recognise and name external parts of the body.	Pupils should have opportunities to: develop body awareness through involvement of all the senses in a wide range of activities.	**Specific body-awareness programmes** Music and movement with an adult – naming and moving or patting parts of the body, clapping, stamping etc. Use large mirrors where appropriate. Massage programmes (*Fun and Games* Denziloe 1994 pp. 51–63) and *Tac Pac*. Music therapy and resonance board sessions.	*Listen and Do* (LDA) Aromatherapy oils (take advice on suitable oils and correct dilution) Resonance board (see information about Beat That! and Soundabout) Tac Pac
		Physical Programmes Motor Education Programmes. Hand function Programmes. Halliwick swimming sessions. Use of the jacuzzi and splash pool. Use of the soft play area and ball pool. Use of large PE apparatus (see *Fun and Games* Denziloe 1994 pp. 63–4 for ideas for body awareness movement).	Interesting objects to hold and explore, trays of things to rattle. Swimming pool, jaccuzzi, splash pool, soft play area, ball pool, slide, physio ball, vibrating toys and mat. *SwitchOn actions* (Brilliant Computing).
		Everyday activities Washing, teeth cleaning, shaving, bathing, hair-washing and drying, dressing, using make-up, washing-up, eating and drinking.	Mirrors, soap, sponge, towel, toothbrush and paste, hairbrush, shampoo, hairdryer, shaving foam, shower, foot spa, nail brush, hand cream, hot and cold water, lipstick, eye shadow, nail varnish
		Art and Craft activities Use of materials with a variety of textures and properties to feel and explore. Body prints.	Paint, clay, dough, glue, paste, crinkly paper, bubble pack, velvet, sandpaper, corrugated paper
		Interactions with others Activities in the dark room – shine torch on faces, hands. Put on shiny clothes. Bells or buttons on gloves, wrists. One to one play with an adult – touch each other's nose, hair, ears. Pull off hats and gloves.	Torches, tinsel wigs, glitter gloves, gloves with bells on, ankle and wrist bells, funny and shiny hats, shiny clothes, face paints

Science Life Processes and Living Things

Objective	POS	Suggested Activities/Strategies	Suggested Resources
NC AT2 Level 1 Pupils recognise and name external parts of plants. They communicate observation of a range of plants in terms of features.	Pupils should have opportunities to: explore a range of plants through each of their senses.	**Smell** Aromatic flowers and plants. Grow a herb garden and use herbs for cooking. Cook with strong smelling vegetables, e.g. onions. Make fruit jam and marmalade. Make lavender bags and pomander balls. Use fruit and herb scented bubble bath. Use scented toiletries such as soap and hand cream. Massage hands with lavender oil (correctly diluted). Concentrate on one fruit for a day, e.g. everything strawberry – colour, smell and taste. **Taste** Grow and taste herbs and cress. Taste raw fruit and vegetables – where suitable. Squeeze juice for drinks or use bought fruit juices. Pupils to help peel and chop fruit and vegetables. Cook and taste each separately. **Touch** Parts of plants with an interesting texture, e.g. bark of tree, furry/smooth leaves, spiky leaves, twigs, conkers, cut fruit, pips and stones. Make bark rubbings and fruit and vegetable prints. Use rubbings, prints, pressed leaves and flowers, bark, straw, twigs, seeds etc. to build up a collage. Plant pips, stones and seeds. **Look at** Flowers etc. through magnifying glass. Sort flowers and vegetables by colour. Grow flowers from seed. Press flowers. Make and use fruit and vegetable dyes. Take part in church or school Harvest Festival. Visit church flower festival.	School grounds and patio Local nature walks Flower pots, soil, seeds, bulbs Gardening tools Art and craft materials Magnifying glasses Nursery catalogues Cooking equipment Onion and herb soups Fruit squash Strawberry and banana milk shake Large pans for dye Juicer and liquidiser Splash pool and foot spa Floral and herbal toiletries Essential oils (follow advice on safe oils and correct dilution) Scented candles Outings to: Garden centres Arboretums Botanical Gardens Greenhouses The Body Shop or similar cosmetics shops Church festivals (See *Fun and Games* Denzilo 1994 pp. 73–6 for sensory gardens as a multisensory experience, and the Sensory Garden package in TFH.)

Science   Life Processes and Living Things

Objective	POS	Suggested Activities/Strategies	Suggested Resources
NC AT2 Level 1 Pupils recognise and identify a range of common animals in terms of features.	Pupils should have opportunites to: experience and explore a range of animals through their senses.	**Smell** Wet fur. Smells in different animal houses. **Feel** Animal fur. Skin of reptiles such as snakes and lizards. Shells of snails and tortoises. Eggs. Insects which can be placed on pupils' bodies. Changes of temperature in animal houses. **Look at** Large and small animals in real life, in pictures, and in photos (especially their own pets), on TV and on CD ROM. Encourage pupils to look at and feel where appropriate, eyes, mouth, teeth, ears and tails of animals. **Listen to** Animal noises in real life. Tape recordings of animal noises – especially relevant if sounds of their pets are recorded and shown alongside photos. Animal noises on CD ROM or TV programmes. **NB** animals which are brightly coloured and noisy such as parrots or myna birds, or animals with a lot of movement, e.g. bats in a bathouse, will evoke the strongest response.	Small animals brought into school (local garden centres may be pleased to do this if requested or pupils could bring in own small pets) Insects in patio and school grounds Magnifying glass Pieces of fur and leather Books and photos CD ROMS Tape recorder TV Animal Soundtracks (LDA) Outdoor sounds – Animal and Birds (Winslow) Visits to: Local nurseries (reptiles, fish, birds, small animals) Wildlife parks and farms Zoos Local natural history museum Taxidermist Pet shop Pupils' homes to see pets **NB** Horse riding provides a truly multisensory activity.

Science   Materials and their Properties

Objective	POS	Suggested Activities/Strategies	Suggested Resources
NC AT3 Level 1 Pupils know about range of properties, (for example, texture, appearance) and communicate observations of materials in terms of these properties.	Pupils should have opportunities to: experience and be aware of contrasts of shape, colour, texture, weight and temperature in planned, structured programmes; experience and participate in activities which cause materials to change.	Follow activities suggested under Science pages 83 and 84. Use the topic in operant term to concentrate on particular concepts such as: hot/cold　　　rough/smooth wet/dry　　　shiny/dull hard/soft　　　solid/liquid light/dark　　　big/small transparent/opaque　old/new heavy/light　　　rigid/bendy Provide activities which give pupils the chance to notice changes in materials when they mix, heat, cool, dissolve, melt, boil and freeze. Build learning objectives into timetabled programmes such as: Physiotherapy sessions, hand group activities, art, swimming, cookery, ICT, darkroom activities, gardening. (see Longhorn 1995 and 1997b). Plan outings which will help to reinforce these concepts and give pupils the opportunity to experience them in a wider context.	See resources listed on Science p. 84 Sensory drama Bonfire parties Hydro pool Swimming pool Soft play area and ball pool Cake and bread making Making hot drinks Making popcorn Feeling ice balloons Snow and ice to melt on hands Cornflour and water Salt dough to bake **Visits to** Science museum Other museums Bakery Car factory Ice rink Seaside Fair Cinema Glass blowing factory Chocolate factory Sweet factory Church (stained glass windows)

Science   Physical Processes

Objective	POS	Suggested Activities/Strategies	Suggested Resources
NC AT4 Level 1 Pupils communicate observations of changes in light, sound or movement that result from actions (for example, switching on a simple electrical circuit, pushing and pulling objects). They recognise that sound and light come from a variety of sources and name some of these.	Pupils should have opportunities to: feel and participate in push and pull movements with their whole bodies;	Rock on floor with an adult or in hammock, rocking chair, rocking horse. Swing in regular swing or blanket. Roll on floor or on physio ball. Pull on blanket, truck, cart. Go down slide, slide on sledge. Fly kites.	Mats/carts to pull Blankets to swing Kites – bought or home made Physio ball Sledge Hammock/swing (see TFH catalogue) Ball pool and soft play equipment – (TFH and Early Learning Centre).
	explore equipment which produces light, sound or movement when pushed or pulled;	Provide mobiles etc. for pupils to explore. Place pupil on resonance board to enhance sounds made when objects are moved by hands or feet. Roll wheeled or round objects down a slope or along the floor, e.g. shiny balls, balls with bells inside, noisy cars. Introduce electrical equipment which responds to small movements such as the sound beam, touch screen or vibrating toys. Progress to computer switch programs and switched toys and equipment. Give pupils opportunities to operate lights, household equipment and cookery appliances from the mains switch and to notice changes in light, sound and movement.	Musical toys with pull cord Shiny balloons Computer programs such as the Switch On series and the Touch Games series (Brilliant Computing from SEMERC) and Blob for Windows from Widgit Sound sensitive programs such as Speak Up and Speak Up Too (Sensory Software from Inclusive Technology) Sound activated equipment and toys (see TFH for crab, toucan, parrot, magic mushroom, mobile, bubble column, Krackle tube etc.) (See *Fun and Games* Denzlioe 1994 pp. 100–1 for ideas for making things happen.)
	experience and use electrical equipment in a wide range of contexts.	On local walks and outings be aware of opportunities for pupils to notice and use equipment where possible, e.g. control on traffic lights, lift call button, automatic doors, escalators.	Outings to discos, funfair, factories, supermarket checkout, large stores

Sample record keeping sheet

SUBJECT: ENGLISH – SPEAKING AND LISTENING
NAME: TERM/YEAR:

Learning Targets – these should relate to PoS	Note date, time of day, learning context, adult present, significant reactions, any other comments	For summative purposes at the end of year or key stage							
		P1a	P1b	P2a	P2b	P3a	P3b	P4	P5
To experience and enjoy vocalising									
To vocalise with an intent to communicate									
Conclusion and way forward									

The P Scales are taken from new curriculum guidelines for schools in England and Wales for pupils attaining significantly below age-related expectations. At the time of writing these are at consultation stage only and the level descriptions P1(a)–P3(b) are generic across the scales. These level descriptions are briefly summarised:

P1(a) encounter (reflex responses)
P1(b) awareness (focus, intermittent reactions)
P2(a) respond consistently (reactive responses, show interest, co-active exploration)
P2(b) proactive responses (communicate, recognise, reach out, examine, cooperate, imitate)
P3(a) intentional communication (seek attention, request, choose to participate, sustain concentration, observe, remember)
P3(b) conventional communication (anticipate, initiate, actively explore, take turns, apply, use)

Lancashire County Council have produced an extended version of P Scales (PIVATS) with learning targets for language and literacy, mathematics and personal and social development.

Resources

Music/drama

Soundbeam

For general information on Soundbeam (equipment which enables people with very little movement to play music) contact:

- Tim Swingler, The Soundbeam Project, Unit 3, Highbury Villas, Kingsdown, Bristol. BF2 8BY
  Tel: 0117 9744142 Fax: 0117 9706241
  Email: tim@soundbeam.co.uk   Web: www.soundbeam.co.uk

For training in use of the Soundbeam and the possibility of borrowing it before making a commitment to buy, contact:

- Soundabout Administrator, Ormerod School, Waynflete Road, Oxford OX3 8DD.
  Tel/Fax: 01865 744175

David Jackson is an independent Soundbeam consultant and an interactive performance artist using soundbeams and switches. He works with pupils and staff on performance projects in schools. These projects involve music, dance and drama and there is an emphasis on staff training. Contact:

- David Jackson, 37 Carey Road, Wokingham, Berks RG40 2NP.
  Tel: 0118 9790211
  Email: tonewall@btinternet.com

CARESS (Creating Aesthetically Resonant Environments in Sound) works with children with SLD and PMLD and is currently working on new technology for Soundbeam and developing curriculum materials. Contact:

- Professor Phil Ellis (coordinator), School of Arts, Design and Media, Bede Tower, Ryhope Road, University of Sunderland SR2 7EG.
  Tel: 0191 515 2540
  Email: phil.ellis@sunderland.ac.uk

For further information about projects such as Timespan, Circle of Sound, new technological developments, curriculum materials, and so on, visit the website on: www.icn.co.uk/timespan

Soundbeam can also be obtained from:
- Toys for the Handicapped (TFH) 5–7 Severnside Business Park, Severn Road, Stourport-on-Severn, Worcs DY13 9HT.
  Tel: 01299 827820 Fax: 01299 827035
  Email: tfhhq@globalnet.co.uk

A resonance board can be purchased through Soundabout, who provide on site training in for teachers and carers in the use of interactive music techniques to enable young people with disabilities to enjoy communicating through music and sound. Low technology methods centre round the resonance board and an extensive library of drums, rain sticks and improvised musical instruments. High technology methods make use of the Soundbeam. Contact (for full information about all they can offer) at:
- Soundabout, Ormerod School, Waynflete Road, Oxford OX3 8DD
  Tel/Fax: 01865 744175

A series of poems called 'The Resonance Board', which can be presented using the resonance board on the table as a musical instrument, can be found in Park, K. (2000) *The SLD Experience*, **26**, 24–6. Contact details for Keith Park are given under the heading Interactive storytelling.

'Beat That!' works with the resonance board and a range of musical instruments. It offers a direct means of communication through music and sound which enables people of any age or ability to listen, feel, compose and create music spontaneously, both individually and within a relaxed group atmosphere. The focus is on the African way of making music where there is no concept of getting it wrong and where every contribution is valued. Trainers work with schools, adult education centres, youth groups etc. and offer several training packages for inset and staff training. For further information contact:
- 'Beat That!' 19 Florence Park Road
  Florence Park
  Oxford OX4 3PN
  Tel: 01865 772213 or 01865 351765

Musical activities

A set of materials which offer teachers a framework for making music with pupils with PMLD is *All join in!* (Ockleford. A., ISBN 1-85878-081-0). The set includes a CD with 78 tracks.

A further title, *Music moves: music in the education of children and young people who are visually impaired and have learning disabilities* (Ockleford, A., ISBN 1-85878-152-3), provides a theoretical base from which a range of musical activities can be developed.

Sound moves is a video with a range of ideas for musical activities for learning and living, at school and at home. It is designed to complement *All join in!* and *Music moves*. These are available from:

- The Royal National Institute for the Blind, 224 Great Portland Street, London W1W 5AA.
  Tel: 020 7388 1266 Fax: 020 7388 2034

Musical instruments

A range of percussion instruments, both regular and switch operated, including an electronic organ operated by contact with the skin, rain maker, clatterpillar and zube tube can be found in the Toys for the Handicapped catalogue (address above).

Drama and literacy

There are theatre companies with experience of working with pupils with PMLD. The Oily Cart Company tour with one-off shows and will design days especially for pupils with PMLD. The Interplay Theatre Company tour nationally to schools and other venues with theatre that is accessible across the five senses. An example of their work is 'Song from the Sea', in which the audience is taken on a ride where they can smell the rain, taste the wind, hear the sea and feel the songs. The Ark is a combined arts organisation working mainly with adults and children with PMLD. They explore music making, dance and drama with a wealth of sensory experiences and describe the result as 'Multisensory theatre'.

- The Oily Cart Company Ltd, Smallwood School Annexe, Smallwood Road, London SW17 0TW.
  Tel: 020 8672 6329 Fax: 020 8672 0792
  Email: oilycart@globalnet.co.uk   Web: www.oilycart.org.uk
- Gareth Moss, Company Manager, Interplay Theatre, Armley Ridge Road, Leeds LS12 3LE.
  Tel: 0113 263 8556 Fax: 0113 231 9285
  Email: interplay@pop3.poptel.org.uk
- The Ark, South Hill Parks Arts Centre, Bracknell, Berkshire RG12 7PA.
  Tel: 01344 483311 Fax: 01344 862449

Mencap (123 Golden Lane, London EC1Y 0RT) has a directory of theatre companies working with people with disabilities. Among these, the following claim to work with people with PMLD 'within the wider services provided':

- Chicken Shed Theatre Company, Tel: 020 8351 6161

- Mind the Gap, Tel: 01274 544 683
- Stackpole Trust Centre, Tel: 01646 661425
- Orpheus Centre, Tel: 01883 744664, Email: staff@orpheus.org.uk

Resources that are out of production, but worth looking for are:
Galaxies and Seaside which were produced by a company called Consortium, which no longer exists.

Puppets

A useful book is *The Knowhow Book of Puppets: A Simple Guide to Making and Working Puppets* by Violet Philpott and Mary Jean McNeil (1975), published by Usborne. Fluppets are realistic animal puppets which are available from toyshops. A large puppet which can be used to encourage communication skills is Molly, available from LDA (catalogue on request); her features enable mouth shapes, tongue positioning and finger movements for signing. Three other puppets, available from Creative Communicating, can be used to support Storytime activities. They are Forgetful Puppet – a full body bear puppet with velcro sensitive hands (31 inches tall); Bobby – a full body Hispanic boy puppet (approximately 21 inches tall); and (another) Molly – a full body girl puppet (approximately 21 inches tall). The Jumbo Puppet Gang (girl, boy and monkey puppet) can be bought as a set or individually from Winslow.

For inexpensive glove puppets visit your local Early Learning Centre or contact them on:

- Early learning Centre,
  Tel: 08705 352253
  Web: www.elc.co.uk

For Inset in schools and information about courses at the London School of Puppetry, contact Caroline Astell-Burt, Tel: 020 7359 7357

The Puppet Centre Trust is a national resource centre for anything to do with puppetry or animation. The Centre publishes *The Directory of Professional Puppeteers: Animations*, a quarterly magazine of puppetry and related theatre, and an education resource pack with hints for making and using puppets, for using puppetry to implement the National Curriculum, and a list of places to visit or contact. In addition school visits to the centre can be arranged for either making or animating puppets (wheelchair access); they also offer displays for schools to borrow, access to a reference library, support for events, and periodical residencies in schools, particularly in the area of special needs. Contact them at:

- BAC, Lavender Hill, Battersea, London SW11.
  Tel: 020 7228 5335 Fax: 020 7228 8863
  Email: pct@puppetcentre.demon.co.uk

Access to books for pupils with sensory impairment

Wordless picture books, easy picture books and picture books for teenagers may be obtained from:
- REACH National Advice Centre for Children with Reading Difficulties, California Country Park, Nine Mile Ride, Finchampstead, Berkshire RG40 4HT.
  Tel: 0118 973 7575, helpline: 08456 040414
  Fax: 0118 973 7105
  Email: reach@reach-reading.demon.co.uk   Web: www.reach-reading.co.uk

Multisensory and tactile stories are available from the following publishers:
- Bag Books, 60 Walham Grove, London SW6 1QR.
  Tel/Fax: 020 7385 4021
  Email: bagbooks@appleonline.net
- Tango Books. 4C/D West Point, 36/37 Warple Way, London W3 0RG
  Tel: 020 8746 1171 Fax: 020 8746 1170
  Email: sales@tangobooks.co.uk

Living Books (from Broderbund) are interactive talking books on CD ROM. Pages can be turned by hitting the space bar or a simple switch, and use of a mouse, touch screen or scan and switch will activate areas of the screen to see or hear something happening. A few of the Living Books series are available from Inclusive Technology; otherwise they are obtainable from:
- REM (Rickitt Educational Media), Great Western House, Langport, Somerset TA 10 9YU.
  Tel: 01458 254700

Lilly and Cogo (Jaritz, Hyvarinen and Schaden) is a Swedish programme, designed especially for children who have low vision, which has short, slow moving stories involving children with familiar objects. Associated dolls and picture books help children to attach meaning to what they see on the screen. Details from:
- Olga Miller, RNIB Education Centre, 224 Great Portland Street, London W1W 5AA.
  Tel: 020 7388 1266 Fax: 020 7388 2034

Interactive storytelling

The following list of interactive storytelling texts has been supplied by Keith Park. (He can be contacted by telephone on 0771 502 6354 or email at kpark@busheyhillrd.demon.co.uk for further information.)
Grove, N. and Park, K. (1996) *Odyssey Now*. London: Jessica Kingsley.
Grove, N. and Park, K. (1999) *Romeo and Juliet: A Multisensory Approach*. London: Bag Books.

Park, K. (1998) 'Dickens for All: Inclusive Approaches to Literature for Children with Sensory and Profound Learning Disabilities', *British Journal of Special Education* **23** (3), 114–18 (for a version of A Christmas Carol).

Park, K. (1998) Theory of Mind and Drama Games: the Point of Little Red Riding Hood', *SLD Experience* **22**, 2–5 (for three drama games).

Park, K. (1999) 'Riverrun and Pricking Thumb: the Use of Poetry', *SLD Experience* **25**, 11–13 (includes poetry by T. S. Eliot, James Joyce and William Shakespeare).

Park, K. (1999) 'Storytelling with People with Sensory Impairments and Additional Disabilities', *SLD Experience* **23**, 17–21 (for versions of Cinderella and A Christmas Carol).

For younger pupils with PMLD

Most books suitable for young children could be adapted. The Book People Ltd have good offers and it is worth obtaining a catalogue (Tel: 0870 6077780)

For teenagers and adults

For this age group literature will have to be adapted, and the above list of interactive storytelling publications contains much material which is suitable for older pupils. *Literature for All* by Nicola Grove (1998), published by David Fulton suggests ways of adapting stories and poetry such as: *Far from the Madding Crowd*; *The Hound of the Baskervilles*; *Kubla Khan* and *Gulliver's Travels*. There are lovely ideas for presenting adult poetry to this age group to include: *Red Boots On* (Kit Wright); *Overheard on a Saltmarsh* (H. H. Munroe); *The Strange Guest* (traditional Scottish) and *Wind* (Ted Hughes).

Grove (1998) suggests the following texts with adaptations for pupils with special needs and these would offer a good starting point for further sensory input for pupils with PMLD:

Romeo and Juliet, Macbeth, A Midsummer Night's Dream from Cutting Edge Publications, 26 Haytor Drive, Milber, Newton Abbot, South Devon TQ12 4DU; *Danny the Champion of the World, Shakespeare for All* packs (available from Questions Publishing, 27 Frederick Street, Hockley, Birmingham B1 3HH); The Graphic Shakespeare Series: *Julius Caesar, Romeo and Juliet, Macbeth*, retold by Hilary Burningham (Evans Brothers).

Further poetry which could be adapted for teenagers and adults includes *Strawberry Drums*, a book of poems put together by Adrian Mitchell (published by Simon and Schuster) an amusing and well illustrated collection of poems with a beat, suitable for older pupils, and:

The Nation's 100 Favourite poems (1996) – book and cassette. London: BBC books.

Heaney, S. and Hughes, T. (1992) *The Rattle Bag*. London: Faber.
Heaney, S. and Hughes, T. (1997) *The School Bag*. London: Faber.
Douglas, J. (1996) *Poems Deep and Dangerous*. Cambridge University Press.
For more ideas for access to literature for pupils with PMLD, see Figures 8.1, 8.2 and 8.3 in Chapter 8

Multisensory environment

The Toys for the Handicapped (TFH) catalogue has a wide range of equipment and toys for all ages. Small *visual* equipment includes: laser wand, glitter tube, diffraction papers. Fluorescent materials and toys include: UV lamp; UV lantern; roly poly drum; rotating mobile; magnetic board with fluorescent shapes; line light tubing; line light panel; bead pockets; bead tubes; balls; body straps; wall padding; paint.

The catalogue also features a projection tent – a netting tent for use in a dark room: images can be projected onto the walls from outside to create an intimate space. There is also a back projection screen which is placed between the projector and the client: project onto the back of the screen for a much clearer image.

A cheaper home made version of the above can be created using curtain lining material.

- Toys for the handicapped (TFH), 5–7 Severnside Business Park, Severn Road, Stourport-on-Severn, Worcestershire DY13 9HT.
  Tel: 01299 827820 Fax: 01299 827035
  Email: tfh@tfhuk.com   Web: tfhuk.com

Whole-body sensory stimulation/movement

Tac Pac by Hilary Wainer, Bobbie Storemont and Christine Wright, three half-hour tapes with appropriate tempos and rhythms to accompany specific sensory activities. Pupils can begin to associate certain sounds with sensations as they are fanned, flicked with little mops, 'slapped' with spatulas, stroked with fur fabric, tapped and rolled with chopsticks, brushed with sponges, rolled with bags of marbles, drummed with hands etc. Adults are encouraged to give children a chance to anticipate sensations and to express likes and dislikes. Tac Pac is published by Hammersmith and Fulham Resources for Learning and is available from Christine Marks (see below). *Listen and Do* is a pack of six cassette tapes with 24 ten-minute activities to help children to follow instructions, recognise familiar sounds and sequence sounds. It is available from LDA.

Musical mats, pressure pads etc. are available from Toys for the Handicapped (see previous section).

Inexpensive sound producing mats such as Jungle Crawl Mat (makes jungle sounds) and Funky Footprints are available from the Early Learning Centre (see previous section). Also available from TFH is a wide range of swings, hammocks and accessories designed specifically for people with physical disabilities.

A book of ideas for parachute play with physically able-bodied children is: *Parachute Play* by Liz Wilmes and Dick Wilmes. The book and also a large colourful parachute are available from Winslow.

Suggested reading for Sherborne movement is Sherborne (1990). Further information may be obtained from:

- George and Cindi Hill, 1 The Vale, Pucklechurch, Avon BS16 9NW.
  Tel: 0117 937 3647
- The Sherborne Resource Centre
  Tel/Fax: 01344 625 811
- Tac Pac, Christine Marks, Newdigate House, Church Hill, Harefield, Middlesex UB9 6DX.
- Learning Development Aids (LDA)
  Tel: 01945 463441 Fax: 01945 587361
  Web: www.instructionalfair.co.uk
- Winslow
  Tel: 01869 244644 Fax: 01869 32004
  Web: www.winslow.press.co.uk

Play and leisure

Toys, play materials and activities

The following titles are useful:

Denziloe, J. (1994) *Fun and Games: Practical Leisure Ideas for People with Profound Disabilities.* Oxford: Butterworth-Heinemann.

Lear, R. (1977) *Play Helps.* London: Heinemann Medical. (4th edition available from Winslow.)

Lear, R. (1990) *More Play Helps.* London: Heinemann Medical.

Lear, R. (1991) *Do it Yourself.* London: The National Association of Toy and Leisure Libraries/Play Matters.

Lear, R. (1996) *Play Helps: Toys and Activities for Children with Special Needs.* Oxford: Butterworth-Heinemann.

Toys for the Handicapped produce switch operated and sound sensitive toys including vibrating toys such as snakes; jiggy piggy; hairbrush; vibro grip; vibro tube. They offer a selection of balls incuding: crystal sponge ball (sparkles and flashes); koosh ball; squidgy ball; bumpy ball; spider ball; wobble mine (wobbles and rotates at high speed); fluorescent balls and large clear jingle ball with bells inside. Early Learning Centre stores are also good sources. For small, inexpensive play items the Stocking fillas catalogue is useful. Items include: optical prism, animal ball (playful weasel), wailing UFO top, clockwork mouse, diving dolphin, glitter putty, ghost ball, stress relief ball (soft and malleable), glow window paint, signal flash torch, 4-colour torch, aquarium hot water bottle (transparent with floating fish), colour change yo-yo, bag of laughs, ghostly glow make-up, fantastic taste kit, flashing earrings, flashing bow tie, Rudolph bells (to wear on wrist or ankle), whistle lips. Catalogues from:

- Toys for the Handicapped
  Tel: 01299 827820 Fax: 01299 827035
  Email: tfh@tfhuk.com
- Early Learning Centres
  Tel: 08705 352352
  Web: www.elc.co.uk
- Stocking fillas
  Tel: 0870 908 7040
  Web: www.stockingfillas.co.uk

Associations for play and leisure

The National Association of Toy and Leisure Libraries' member groups promote play and learning by providing information, publications and training for parents, carers and professionals.

Information on toys appropriate to need (i.e. multicultural and special needs), and the whereabouts of local toy and leisure libraries. Also information about how to start up and run a new toy and leisure library.

Publications and toy guides to chose the right toy for the children, including:

- 'Hear and Say' – toys and play for children with visual impairment;
- 'Switch into Action' – demonstrating how to increase the play potential of toys and equipment for children with special needs by adding simple switch devices;
- 'Playsense' – a play resource for babies and young children covering development through thinking and imaginative play, belonging and connecting, and language and movement play.

Training: Day courses on play and all running toy and leisure libraries are held regularly around the country. Accredited training and national conferences.

- The National Association of Toy and Leisure Libraries, 68 Churchway, London NW1 1LT.
  Tel: 020 7387 9592 Fax: 020 7383 2714
  Email: admin@natll.ukf.net   Web: www.charitynet.org/~NATLL

Action for Leisure (formerly PLANET) is a small national charity working to promote play, leisure and recreation with and for disabled adults and children. They offer a resource and information centre with a database of information about toys and materials to buy, information about suppliers, videos, books etc.

- Action for Leisure, c/o Warwickshire College, Moreton Morrell Centre, Moreton Morrell, Warwickshire CV35 9BL
  Tel: 01926 650195 Fax: 01296 650104

Information about adventure playgrounds for disabled children, publications, training and advice about setting up and running inclusive play facilities etc. is available from:

- Kidsactive, (Joanna Ryam, Service Manager), Pryor's Bank, Bishop's Park, London SW6 3LA.
  Tel: 020 7731 1435 Fax: 020 7731 4426

Ideas and advice for organising museum trips for pupils with special needs can be found in Pearson and Aloysius (1994) *The Big Foot: Museums and Children with Learning Difficulties* published by British Museum Publications.

Signing and symbols

For information on the Makaton Vocabulary Development Project (for materials and training in the use of signing and symbols) contact:

- Makaton Vocabulary Development Project, 31 Firwood Drive, Camberley, Surrey GU15 3QD.
  Tel/Fax: 01276 61390
  Email: mvdp@makaton.org   Website: http//www.makaton.org

Other useful materials are the *Makaton National Curriculum Resource Vocabulary Series*, consisting of Nursery Rhyme Sign and Sing Books, Makaton Databases and Makaton Make and Do; and Mayer-Johnson's *Picture Communication Symbols* (PCS), which includes symbol sets, folders and pocket books. (This is also available as a software package called *Boardmaker for Windows*.) Both are available from Winslow.

The Symbols Project issues a project pack with information about how people in the project used symbols, how a computer can help with symbols and how other people are using symbols. Contact:

- Sally Paveley, The Symbols Project, The Advisory Unit, 126 Great North Road, Hatfield, Herts AL9 5JZ.
  Tel: 01707 266714
  Story/symbol packs may be obtained from:
- CALL Centre, Faculty of Education, The University of Edinburgh, Paterson's Land, Holyrood Road, Edinburgh EH8 8AQ.
  Tel: 0131 651 6235/6 Fax: 0131 651 6234

Email: CALL.Centre@ed.ac.uk   Web: http://call-centre.cogsci.ed.ac.uk/CallHome

Information Communication Technology

For aids to communication in education contact:

- Ace Centre Advistory Trust, Ace Centre, 92 Windmill Road, Headington, Oxford OX 3 7DR.
  Tel: 01865 763508/759800 Fax: 01865 759800
  Email: ace-centre@ddircon.co.uk

The New Opportunities Fund has provided £230 million of lottery money to train all 45,000 serving teachers of pupils with severe or complex needs in the effective use of ICT. This is being organised by local authorities and will continue until 2003. All Special Schools in England should have been informed directly about this, or information can be obtained from:

- Inclusive Technology Ltd, Saddleworth Business Centre, Huddersfield Road, Delph, Oldham OL3 5DF.
  Tel: 01457 819790
  Fax: 01457 819799
  Email: inclusive@inclusive.co.uk Web: http//www.inclusive.co.uk

or

- SEMERC: Special Needs Learning Network Programme
  Tel: 0161 827 2719
  Email: sis@granadamedia.com   Web: www.semerc.com

Video resources

Hello is a visual stimulation video for children with multiple disabilities who can see light. Sound effects emphasise the movements and patterns. It is produced by the Oxfordshire Visual Impairment Service and available from RNIB. Two other videos with accompanying booklets available from RNIB are:

Making contact: Holistic multi-sensory approaches to communication and
That's what it's all about!: Play, leisure and recreational activities.

For parents and carers

The following organisation produces a directory giving information about rare conditions:

- Contact a Family, 170 Tottenham Court Road, London W1P 0HA.
  Tel: 020 7383 3555

A free helpline for any queries about CP for families and carers is:

- Cerebral palsy helpline
  Tel: 080 8800 3333

Email: cphelpline@scope.org.uk
The listed periodicals (under Periodicals heading) are also helpful and informative for all parents and carers.

Periodicals

PMLD Link, a newsletter written by people working with children and young people with PMLD, provides a forum for discussion, views and information about activities and resources. *Eye Contact* (RNIB) is a journal concerned with the needs of children with impaired vision and additional learning difficulties. *Focus* (RNIB) is a newsletter for staff working with people with visual and learning disabilities. *Talking Sense* is published by Sense, the National Deaf-Blind and Rubella Association, which also provides free factsheets and publications. Contact details can be found below under Suppliers and other useful addresses.

Miscellaneous equipment

Magnetic tape can be obtained from Mike Ayres and Co., Rompa, Toys for the Handicapped, or local stationers. Self-adhesive mirror roll is available from Home Free Tel: 0804 4564545, and convex plastic mirrors from branches of IKEA.

Suppliers and other useful addresses

- ALL (Accreditation of Life and Living), OCR (Oxford Cambridge and RSA Examinations), Westwood Way, Coventry CV4 8JQ.
  Tel: 024 7642 1944 Fax: 024 7642 1944
  Email: cib@ocr.org.uk   Web: www.ocr.org.uk
- ASDAN Award Scheme, ASDAN Central Office, 27 Redland Hill, Bristol BS6 6UX.
  Tel: 0117 946 6228 Fax: 0117 946 766
  Email:asdan@uwe.ac.uk   Web: asdan.co.uk
- 'Beat That!', 19 Florence Park Road, Florence Road, Oxford OX4 3PN
  Tel: 01865 772213 or 01865 351765
- The Booksellers Association, Minster House, 272 Vauxhall Bridge Road, London SW1 1BA.
  Tel: 020 7834 5477
- Cambridge Adaptive Communication (CAC), The Mount, Toft, Cambridge CB3 7RL.
  Tel: 01223 264 24 Fax: 01223 264 254
  Email: info@camad.demon.co.uk   Web: www.camad.demon.co.uk

- Catalyst Education Resources Ltd, 1A Potters Cross, Wootton, Bedfordshire MK43 9JG.
  Tel/Fax: 01234 764108
  Email: Longhorn@village.uunet.lu (for Flo Longhorn's publications)
- Creative Communicating, PO Box 3358, Park City, UT 84060, USA.
  Tel: (435) 645 7737
  Web: www.creative-comm.com
- Crick Computing, 123 The Drive, Northampton NN1 4SW.
  Tel: 01604 713686 Fax: 01604 458333
  Email: crickcomputing@cix.compulink.co.uk
- Foundation for Conductive Education, National Institute for Conductive Education, Cannon Hill House, Russell Road, Moseley, Birmingham B13 8RD.
  Tel: 0121 449 1569 Fax: 0121 449 1611
  Email: Foundation@conductive-education.org.uk
- Greenwich Visual Impairment Service, Greenwood School, Welton Road, Greenwich, London SE 18 2JD.
  Tel: 020 8316 1068
- Inclusive Technology Ltd, Saddleworth Business Centre, Huddersfield Road, Delph, Oldham OL3 5DF.
  Tel: 01457 819799 Fax: 01457 819799
  Email: inclusive@inclusive.co.uk   Web: http://www.inclusive.co.uk
- Learning Development Aids (LDA), Duke Street, Wisbech, Cambs PE13 2AE.
  Tel: 01945 463441 Fax: 01945 587361
  Web: www.instructionalfair.co.uk
- Liberator Ltd, Whitegates, Swinstead, Lincolnshire NG33 4PA.
  Tel: 01476 550391 Fax: 01476 550357
- Mayer Johnson Co. (available in UK from CAC)
  PO Box 1579, Solana Beach, CA 92075 7579, USA.
  Tel: (800) 588-4548 Fax:(619) 550 0449
- Mencap, 123 Golden Lane, London EC 1Y ORT.
  Tel: 020 7454 0454
  Web: www.mencap.org
- The Children's Play Information Service, The National Children' Bureau, 8 Wakeley Street, London, EC1V 7QE
  Tel: 020 7843 6303
- *PMLD Link* for subscriptions or back copies contact Carol Ouvry, editor, The Old Rectory, Hope Mansell, Ross-on-Wye, Herefordshire HR9 5TL
  Tel: 01989 750382
  Email: PMLD@mansell.wyenet.co.uk
- QED 2000, 1 Prince Alfred Street, Gosport, Hampshire PO12 1QH.
  Tel: 0870 787 8850 Fax: 0870 787 8860

Email: sales@QEDLtd.com

- Qualification and Curriculum Authority (QCA) (for curriculum enquiries contact Nick Peacey), 29 Bolton Street, London W1Y 7PD.
  Tel: 020 7509 6666
  Email: peaceyn@qca.org.uk   Web: www.qca.org.uk
- REM (Rickitt Educational Media), Great Western House, Langport, Somerset TA10 9YU.
  Tel: 01458 254700
- The Royal National Institute for the Blind, 224 Great Portland Street, London W1W 5AA.
  Tel: 020 7388 1266 Fax: 020 7388 2034
  For catalogues and book orders: RNIB, PO Box 173, Peterborough, PE2 6WS
  Tel: 08457 023153 Fax: 01733 371555
- SEMERC, Granada Learning, Granada Television, Quay Street, Manchester M60 9EA.
  Tel: 0161 827 2927 Fax: 0161 827 2966
  Email: semerc.sales@granadamedia.com   Web: www.semerc.com
- Sense, The National Deaf-Blind and Rubella Association, 11–13 Clifton Terrace, Finsbury Park, London N4 3SR.
  Tel/Fax: 020 7272 7774
  Email: enquiries@sense.org.uk   Web: www.sense.org.uk
- 'Soundabout', Ormerod School, Waynflete Road, Oxford OX3 8DD.
  Tel/Fax: 01865 744175
- Tash International Inc. (available in Britain through CAC)
  Unit 1, 91 Station Street, Ajax, Ontario, Canada L1S 3H2.
  Tel: 800 463 5685 Fax: 905 686 6895
  Email: tashcan@aol.com   Web: www.tashint.com
- Toys for the Handicapped (TFH), 5–7 Severn Fine Business Park, Severn Road, Stourport-on-Severn, Worcestershire DY13 9QB.
  Tel: 01299 878512 Fax: 01299 827035
  Email: tfhhq@globalnet.co.uk
- Widgit Software Ltd, 102 Radford Road, Leamington Spa, CV31 1LF.
  Tel: 01926 885303 Fax: 01926 885293
  Email: literacy@widgit.com   Web: http://www.widgit.com
- Winslow, Telford Road, Bicester, Oxon OX6 0TS.
  Tel: 01869 244644 Fax: 01869 32004
  Email: info@winslow.press.co.uk   Web:www.winslow.press.co.uk

Glossary of terms

Attainment Targets (ATs) Attainment Targets lay down the expected standards for pupils in terms of Level or end of Key Stage descriptions for each core and foundation subject of the National Curriculum.

Ball pool A pool shape filled with 2.75 inch diameter plastic balls in which children can move, roll, sink, throw, explore etc.

Beat That! A small company working with the resonance board and a range of musical instruments. It offers a direct means of communication through music and sound which enables people of any age or ability to listen, feel, compose and create music spontaneously, both individually and within a relaxed group atmosphere.

BIGmack A switch device with 20 seconds of memory. It allows a message to be recorded and played back when pressed.

Canon Ion still video camera A camera which stores up to 50 still video images on a magnetic disc. The images can be viewed through the television and can be erased and the disc can be re-used. There are no processing costs.

Cerebral palsy A general term for a wide range of non-progressive brain disorders which result in some sort of movement impairment. Associated difficulties may include sensory or perceptual impairment, learning difficulties and epilepsy.

Code of Practice (on the identification and assessment of special educational needs) Guidance for LEA's and governing bodies of schools on their duties in relation to statemented and unstatemented pupils with special educational needs.

Co-located sites Special schools on mainstream sites, but maintaining their own separate units.

Comboard (tash) A picture symbol communication board with a motor-driven pointer, operated by pressing a single switch.

Conductive Education A system of educating children with motor disorders in order to establish 'orthofunction'. Devised and developed in Hungary by Andras Peto in the period following the Second World War.

Core subjects English, mathematics and science in the National Curriculum for England.

Department of Education and Employment (DfEE) Central government department with the responsibility for providing education in schools in England.

E-Tran Frame A wooden picture frame with a transparent centre. Objects, pictures or symbols can be attached to the perimeter. Adult sits opposite the child and can see where the pupil's eyes are pointing.

Halliwick swimming method A method for teaching the disabled to swim, devised by James McMillan who began the work in 1949. Each 'swimmer' works with an instructor, no buoyancy aids are used and independent movement is encouraged. Groups are run by a leader and control in the water is learned through a variety of games, involving the use of songs and stories and small equipment such as balls, sponges and quoits.

Individual Education Plan (IEP) Pupils with special educational needs should have an IEP which identifies the nature of the learning difficulties, action to be taken, staff involved, teaching programmes and resources, timescale for identified targets to be achieved and arrangements for assessing and reviewing.

Key Stages (KS) Stages in each pupil's education to which elements of the National Curriculum apply: KS1 (from start of compulsory education to age 7); KS2 (7–11); KS3 (11–14); KS4 (14 to the end of compulsory education).

Little house of Lilli Nielsen A perspex box with a system for hanging interchangeable everyday objects for children to locate and explore.

Motor Education Programmes Exercise programmes based on the principles of Conductive Education.

National Curriculum (NC) The core and foundation subjects along with their attainment targets and programmes of study.

National Curriculum Council (NCC) An advisory body on aspects of the curriculum in schools. These responsibilities were taken over by SCAA in October 1993.

National Literacy Strategy and **National Numeracy Strategy** Frameworks for improving standards of literacy and numeracy in primary schools in England, introduced by the Department for Education and Employment (1998 and 1999).

Objects of reference An 'object of reference' is an object that has a particular meaning associated with it. The emphasis is on perceptual rather than cognitive abilities.

Programmes of Study (PoS) These set the minimum statutory entitlement to the knowledge, understanding and skills for each subject and at each key stage of the NC.

Qualifications and Curriculum Authority (QCA) A non-ministerial government office offering advice to the DfEE on the content and impact of the National Curriculum.

Records of Achievement (RoA) More than a summative record of educational attainments, these are intended to give evidence of a pupil's interests and hobbies and to reflect a holistic approach to assessment. At the core of the process is pupil involvement in developing and owning their own records.

Resonance board A slightly raised board capable of taking the weight of people sitting or lying on it. Any small movement creates resonance under the child and produces a magnified sound.

School Curriculum and Assessment Authority (SCAA) The advisory body for all aspects of the curriculum to include assessment and examinations.

Sherborne movement Relationship play which can be developed through developmental movement. Much work is done in pairs with an emphasis on sensing each other's movements, building confidence and working together as a partnership.

SLD: severe learning difficulties and **PMLD: profound and multiple learning difficulties** Pupils with these combined degrees of intellectual impairment account for approximately two per cent of pupil population.

Soft play area A purpose built environment with padded walls and soft play shapes in bright colours.

Soundabout A company formed by professionals with a musical background and experience of visual impairment. On-site training is provided for teachers and carers in the use of interactive music techniques to enable young people with disabilities to enjoy communicating through music and sound. Low technology methods centre round the resonance board and an extensive library of drums, rain sticks and improvised musical instruments. High technology methods make use of the soundbeam.

Soundbeam A piece of equipment which enables people with very little movement to play music. Any movements within the invisible beam 'play' the electronic keyboard. New developments enable it to be linked to various multisensory effects or to a vibrating board.

Special Educational Needs (SEN) Refers to pupils who for a range of reasons have learning difficulties which are significantly greater than those of the majority of pupils of the same age.

Switch controlled devices Any electrical or adapted battery powered device to which a special switch has been connected. Switches can be operated by movement, touch or sound.

Symbol system The following pictographic symbol systems are those most commonly used for pupils with PMLD:

- *Makaton:* based on the British Sign Language but adapted for use with people with learning disabilities. Almost all the symbols are the same as the Rebus symbols. Designed to allow access to the National Curriculum.
- *Rebus:* a glossary of about 950 clear, simple symbols.
- *Picture Communication Symbols (PCS):* one of the largest picture symbol sets available today, consisting of over 3,000 symbols in black, white and colour. Simple, clear drawings are easily recognised.

Tac Pac Tapes with appropriate tempos and rhythms to accompany specific sensory activities. The pack is described in the Whole body sensory stimulation/ movement section of Resources (Part 2).

Touchscreen A screen which is mounted externally on the monitor. Appropriate software allows it to emulate the mouse.

Waldon method An approach developed by Geoffrey Waldon and focusing on children with learning difficulties, in particular those with autistic behaviour. The rationale of this approach is to provide the child with a range of experiences which will enable him or her to acquire the 'learning to learn' tools normally gained through undirected play in the first years of life.

Bibliography

Aherne, P. and Thornber, A. (1990) *Communication for All.* London: David Fulton Publishers.

Aitken, S. and Buultjens, M. (1992) *Vision for Doing: Assessing Functional Vision of Learners who are Multiply Disabled.* Edinburgh: Moray House Publications.

Barber, M. (1994) 'Contingency awareness: Putting research into the classroom', in Coupe O'Kane, J. and Smith, B. (eds) *Taking control: Enabling People with Learning Difficulties,* 49–59. London: David Fulton Publishers.

Bentley, T. (2000) 'Learning for a creative age', in Crake, P. and Johnson, M. (eds) *Education Futures: Lifelong Learning,* 17–21. London: Design Council/RSA.

Berger, A. *et al.* (1999) *Implementing the Literacy Hour for Pupils with Learning Difficulties.* London: David Fulton Publishers.

Berger, A. *et al.* (2000) *Implementing the National Numeracy Strategy for Pupils with Learning Difficulties: Access to the Daily Mathematics Lesson.* London: David Fulton Publishers.

Brown, N. *et al.* (1998) 'Sensory Needs', in Lacey, P. and Ouvry, C. (eds) *People with Profound and Multiple Learning Difficulties: A Collaborative Approach to Meeting Complex Needs,* 29–38. London: David Fulton Publishers.

Carpenter, B. (1994) 'Facing the Future: the challenge of educating learners with profound and multiple learning difficulties', *Westminster Studies in Education* 17, 37–43.

Collis, M. and Lacey, P. (1996) *Interactive Approaches to Teaching: A Framework for Inset.* London: David Fulton Publishers.

Dale, F. J. (1990) *The Stimulation Guide.* Hemel Hempstead: Woodhead-Faulkner.

Denziloe, J. (1994) *Fun and Games: Practical Leisure Ideas for People with Profound Disabilities.* Oxford: Butterworth-Heinemann.

DES (1989) *National Curriculum: From Policy to Practice.* London: DES.

DFE (1994) *Code of Practice on the Identification and Assessment of Special Educational Needs.* London: HMSO.

DFE (1995) *The National Curriculum.* London: HMSO.

DfEE (1998) *The National Literacy Strategy: Framework for Teaching.* Sudbury: DfEE Publications.

DfEE (1999) *The National Numeracy Strategy: Framework for teaching mathematics from Reception to Year 6.* Sudbury: DfEE Publications.

DfEE/QCA (1998) *Supporting the Target Setting Process: Guidance for effective target setting for pupils with special educational needs.* Nottingham: DfEE Publications Centre.

DfEE/QCA (1999) *The National Curriculum: Handbook for Primary teachers in England, Key Stages 1 and 2.* London: DfEE/QCA.

Fagg, S. *et al.* (1990) *Science for All.* London: David Fulton Publishers.

Fawkes, S. *et al.* (eds) (1999) *Using Television and Video to Support Learning: A Handbook for Teachers in Special Education and Mainstream Schools.* London: David Fulton Publishers.

Fuller, C. (1990) *Tactile Stories: A Do-it-yourself Guide to Making Six Tactile Books.* London: Resources for Learning Difficulties.

Gardner, L. (1999) 'Making a Splash' *Theatre First*, **4**, 4–5.

Gerber, M. M. (1995) 'Inclusion at the high-water mark? Some thoughts on Zigmond and Baker's case studies of inclusive educational programs', *Journal of Special Education* **29** (2), 181–91.

Goleman, D. (1996) *Emotional Intelligence.* London: Bloomsbury Press.

Grove, N. (1998) *Literature for All: Developing Literature in the Curriculum for Pupils with Special Educational Needs.* London: David Fulton Publishers.

Grove, N. and Park, K. (1996) *Odyssey Now.* London: Jessica Kingsley.

Grove, N. and Peacey, N. (1999) 'Teaching subjects to pupils with profound and multiple learning difficulties', *British Journal of Special Education* 26 (2), 83–86.

Heimel, C. (1983) 'Lower Manhattan Survival Tactics', *Village Voice.*

Katz, L. (2000) 'Starting them young: the learning experience', in Crake, P. and Johnson, M. (eds) *Education Futures: Lifelong Learning*, 62–3. London: Design Council/RSA.

Kiernan, C. C. and Reid, B. (1987) *Pre-verbal Communication Schedule.* Windsor: NFER/Nelson.

Lewis, A. (1995) *Primary Special Needs and the National Curriculum* (2nd edition). London: Routledge.

Longhorn, F. (1993a) *Prerequisites to Learning for Very Special People.* Wootton, Beds: Catalyst Education Resources.

Longhorn, F. (1993b) *Sensory Science – National Curriculum for Very Special People.* Wootton, Beds: Catalyst Education Resources.

Longhorn, F. (1995) *A Sensory Curriculum for Very Special People.* London: Souvenir Press.

Longhorn, F. (1996/7. 'A Sensory Challenge', *PMLD Link*, Winter, **26**, 16–17.

Longhorn, F. (1997a) *Enhancing Education Through the Use of Ultraviolet Light and Fluorescing Materials: Resource Pack*. Wootton, Beds: Catalyst Education Resources Ltd.

Longhorn, F. (1997b) *Sensory Cookery for Very Special People: A Practical Approach*. Wootton, Beds: Catalyst Education Resources.

Madina, A. (1999) in McCrum, R. (ed.) (1999) *Millenium Experience*. London: The New Millennium Experience Company (NMEC).

Mencap (and Partners) (1999) *Reading for All: Ideas for stories and reading for children and young adults with severe and profound learning disabilities*. Mencap Public Liaison Unit (Tel: 020 7696 5593 – there is a preferential price for parents).

Miller, O. (1999) 'The National Literacy Strategy and pupils with visual impairment and multiple disabilities', *Eye Contact (RNIB)*, Spring, **23** 25–6.

Ouvry, C. (1991) 'Access for Pupils with Profound and Multiple Learning Difficulties', in Ashdown, R. *et al.* (eds) *The Curriculum Challenge*, 41–61. London: Falmer Press.

Ouvry, C. (1998) 'Making Relationships', in Lacey, P. and Ouvry, C. (eds) *People with Profound and Multiple Learning Difficulties: A Collaborative Approach to Meeting Complex Needs*, 29–38. London: David Fulton Publishers.

Ouvry, C. and Mitchell, S. (1995) 'Play Materials', in Hogg, J. and Cavet, J. (eds) *Making Leisure Provision for People with Profound and Multiple Disabilities*, 178–96. London: Chapman and Hall.

Ouvry, C. and Saunders, S. (1996) 'Pupils with Profound and Multiple Learning Difficulties', in Carpenter *et al.* (eds) *Enabling Access: Effective Teaching and Learning for Pupils with Learning Difficulties* 200–17. London: David Fulton Publishers.

Park, K. (1999/2000) 'Reading Objects: Literacy and Objects of Reference', *PMLD Link* **12** (1), 4–9.

Park, K. (2000) 'The Resonance Board', *The SLD Experience* **26**, 24–26.

Peter, M. (1994) *Drama for All*. London: David Fulton Publishers.

Piaget, J. (1952) *The Origins of Intelligence in Children*. New York: International University Press Publications.

QCA/DfEE (1999) 'SEN regional conferences, March 1999', *Special Educational Needs*, Update 2, June, 1–4.

QCA (1999) *The review of the National Curriculum in England: The consultation materials*. London: QCA.

SCAA (1996) *Planning the Curriculum: for pupils with profound and multiple learning difficulties*. London: SCAA Publications.

Sherborne, V. (1990) *Developmental Movement for Children*. Cambridge: Cambridge University Press.

Taylor, M. and Hallgarten, J. (2000) 'Freedom to modernise', in Crake, P. and Johnson, M. (eds) *Education Futures: Lifelong Learning*, 9–13. London: Design Council/RSA.

Thompson, M. (1999) 'Integration links at Frank Wise School', *PMLD Link* **11** (3), 2–6.

Ware, J. (1996) *Creating a Responsive Environment for People with Profound and Multiple Learning Difficulties*. London: David Fulton Publishers.

Winstock, A. (1994) *The Practical Management of Eating and Drinking Difficulties in Children*. Bicester: Winslow.

Index

Page numbers followed by a letter 'r' or 'g' refer to entries in the Resources section or Glossary respectively.